The Little Book of
PUNS

The Little Book of
PUNS

Alison Westwood

canary
press

There's two fish in a tank, and one says 'How do you drive this thing?'

With thanks to Margaret and Lol Briggs
and Tom and Kate Briggs for their contributions

This 2011 edition published by Canary Press
an imprint of Omnipress Limited, UK

ISBN: 978-1-907795-02-2

Canary Press
An imprint of Omnipress Ltd
Chantry House, 22 Upperton Road
Eastbourne, East Sussex BN21 1BF
England

Printed and bound in Malaysia

10 9 8 7 6 5 4 3 2 1

Editor: Jennifer Davies
Production Manager: Benita Estevez
Cover and internal design: Anthony Prudente

CONTENTS

INTRODUCTION

'What have the Romans ever done for us?' asks an irate John Cleese in Monty Python's *Life of Brian*. Well the world's oldest known joke book dates back to Roman times, for starters. Written in Greek in the third or fourth century AD, *Philogelos* – or *The Laughter Lover* to us – contains around 260 one-liners that experts claim are remarkably similar to those of today. The witticisms on its pages would almost certainly have included that much-maligned comic device – the pun.

Since said book was written, puns have divided opinion; embraced by some and dismissed by others. But whether you believe that they are sophisticated linguistic devices that demonstrate the wit of those uttering them, or puerile attempts at humour that prompt eyes to roll and groans to be emitted, they are all around us. They are used in advertising slogans and form the headlines of tabloid newspapers, persuading us to pay for the products they are promoting or to read the news they are announcing. As far as American writer and stickler for the English language, Ambrose Bierce, was concerned, the pun is '... a form of wit, to which wise men stoop and fools aspire.' In fact, looking for quotations in praise of puns is something of a thankless task; throughout their history they have been subjected to some fairly vitriolic attacks by notable literary figures and treated with the same contempt that text message language is today.

Universal Language of Puns

However, since puns were conceived, numerous men and women have made a good living out of using them; Shakespeare's work is littered with them and they form some of the most memorable elements of Oscar Wilde's plays. Perhaps the true beauty of puns is the fact that they are universal. They can be told by anybody and in different ways yet still retain their humour. Tommy Cooper used them as the perfect foil to his deliberately bungled magic tricks along with his trademark chuckle: 'I went to buy some camouflage trousers the other day but I couldn't find any.' While Leslie Nielsen employed a deadpan approach to his delivery, simultaneously making him both the 'straight man' and his silly counterpart: 'Surely you can't be serious?', 'I am serious and don't call me Shirley.' The immortal lines of both of these late greats – and many others like them – still inspire fond laughter and remain as irresistibly quotable as they always have been.

Without wishing to get too academic and overanalyse the deeply serious matter of comedy in hand, it's worth looking at what a pun is. In its simplest form, the pun is a play on words – either on the different senses of a particular word or similar sounding words. Another word for 'pun' is 'paronomasia', a term combining two Greek words, namely 'para' – beside – and onomasia – naming. The Greek will inherit the earth, it would seem. There are two basic kinds of puns, namely homographic and homophonic. Homographic puns exploit the multiple meanings of words with the same spelling, e.g: bear a grudge, polar bear. Their homophonic cousins make use of words that sound the same when spoken despite having different spellings and meanings, eg: jeans and genes, grease and Greece. There are, of course, several other varying types such as those that work on the principle of replacing one sound with another that sounds vaguely similar, for example:

I'm going on a Safari – Kenya believe it?

Like the *Philogelos*, this book is an unashamed celebration of puns; join us now on a journey that takes in the wit and wisdom of some of history's most enlightened wordsmiths. Taking in humour from the sublime to the ridiculous, we hope that in the best traditions of joke-telling, this leaves you laughing.

I used to have a fear of hurdles, but I got over it

WILLIAM SHAKESPEARE

1564–1616

Golden lads and girls all must As chimney sweepers, come to dust

Rival, Robert Greene, badmouthed him aloud,
Yet for Ben Jonson he stood proud
As the 'Soul of the age,
The applause, delight, the wonder of our stage'.
Critic Thomas Rymer had a downer on Good Will,
Tho' John Dryden of the Bard scarce had his fill.

Certain literary historians disowned him, attributing his achievements to the likes of Marlow or Bacon, but the Romantics simply loved him. The Victorians so revered him that George Bernard Shaw denounced their adulation as 'bardolatry'. Then T. S. Eliot – no less – slapped down Shaw, arguing that Shakespeare's 'primitiveness' made his work more, not less, modern. Curiouser and curiouser – Malice in Shakespeareland?

Author and poet Samuel Johnson complained about Shakespeare's frequent use of less serious puns, or 'quibbles': 'A quibble is to Shakespeare what luminous vapours are to the traveller! He follows it to all adventures; it is sure to lead him out of his way, sure to engulf him in the mire. It has some malignant power over his mind, and its fascinations are irresistible.' Samuel Johnson declared the pun 'the lowest form of humour', however, in 1755 he changed his tune judging by the contents of his publication *Dictionary of the English Language*. It was the first serious work of its kind, and was garlanded with a multiplicity of quotations from said playwright, William Shakespeare. Did he, then, quote Shakespeare 'with bated breath', in trepidation at the prospect of facing criticism himself, or did he truly think it 'a foregone conclusion', that by 1800 Shakespeare would be installed as national poet and celebrated as the finest exponent of the English language? Of course, so why the doubting of the puns (not to mention the pouting of the duns)?

An Educated Man

Who was this man, who could both divide and rule and deride and fool? Could it be that his puns enhance the ambience, heighten the drama, intensify the emotions, raise laughter and spirits and make audience and reader alike gasp with admiration at the sheer genius of the wordplay? His biography reveals little in the way of insight into his inspiration, apart, perhaps from his education and marriage. At King's New School, Stratford, he received an intensive education in Latin grammar and classics – explanation enough for his precision with words and for a background to his choice of subject matter and plays, but no more than that. His marriage in 1582, at the age of 18, to 26-year-old Anne Hathaway, was followed six months later by the birth of their first child, Susanna. The birth of twins Hamnet and Judith, in 1585, also offers evidence of his early exposure to love and the responsibilities of parenthood. What else? Well, his father made gloves and traded in wool. His mother, Mary Arden, was the daughter of a well-to-do local landowner. Interesting, but hardly revealing. And then? A seven-year gap, his 'lost years', disclosing nothing, until his reappearance in London in 1592, where he was working in the theatre. Of major significance, however, was the fact that Shakespeare, as both playwright and player, understood and appreciated the benefits of insight from both ends of the performance spectrum: the writer's stunningly perceptive analysis of situation and complex relationships allied to the performer's admiration at the writer's creativity, coupled with a burning desire to realize on the stage the vision so originally cast and expressed on the page.

Playwright and Player

Shakespeare the actor was employed by the Lord Chamberlain's Company, renamed the King's Company in 1603, on the succession of King James. The company acquired interests in two theatres in Southwark, near the banks of the Thames, namely The Globe and The Blackfriars. As a writer, Shakespeare saw his poetry published before his plays, with two poems appearing in 1593 and 1594. He probably also wrote most of his sonnets at this time. Records of his plays first appeared in 1594, and he produced roughly two a year until around 1611. His early plays were mainly comedies and histories, including *Henry VI*, *Titus Andronicus*, *A Midsummer Night's Dream*, *The Merchant of Venice* and *Richard II*. He then wrote mainly tragedies until about 1608, including *Hamlet*, *Othello*, *King Lear*, and *Macbeth*. In his final phase, he wrote tragicomedies, also known as romances, such as *The Tempest*, and he collaborated with other playwrights. Now quite wealthy from the fruits of his writing and performances, though by no means enjoying the elevated status he is now accorded, Shakespeare spent the remainder of his life in Stratford. He died on 23 April 1616 and was buried in Holy Trinity Church in Stratford. The first collected edition of his works, *The First Folio*, was published in 1623. Constructed to highlight the writer's mastery of language, these eloquent witty play on words were in Shakespeare's day the wquivalent of a good punchline.

So, back to puns and Shakespeare. Humorous and non-humorous puns were – and still are – a standard poetic device in English literature, employed by many writers, not least, Shakespeare himself, who is estimated to have used over 3,000 in his plays.

Richard III

Now is the winter of our discontent made glorious summer by this sun* of York
(*son/sun)

Cymbeline

Golden lads and girls all must,
As chimney sweepers, come to dust.

Hamlet

Polonius: Will you walk out of the air*, my lord?
(*draughty room)
Hamlet: Into my grave.*
(*anywhere with anyone but you)

....

Hamlet [to Polonius, his uncle and stepfather]: A little more
than kin, and less than kind.*
(*twice related but paradoxically neither kin nor kindred nor
kindhearted)

....

Claudius: How is it that the clouds still hang on you?
Hamlet: Not so, my lord, I am too much in the sun.*
(*Hamlet feels Claudius has called him 'son' once too often)

....

Hamlet [to Horatio and Marcellus, who try to keep him from
following the Ghost]:
Unhand me, gentlemen,
By heaven! I'll make a ghost of him that lets* me!
(*hinders)

Ophelia [talking about Hamlet with her father]:
He hath, my lord, of late made many tenders*
(*offers)
Of his affection to me.
Polonius: Affection! pooh! you speak like a green girl,
Unsifted in such perilous circumstance.
Do you believe his tenders, as you call them?
Ophelia: I do not know, my lord, what I should think.
Polonius: Marry, I'll teach you: think yourself a baby;
That you have ta'en these tenders* for true pay,
(*legal tender/currency)
Which are not sterling. Tender* yourself more dearly;
(*regard)
Or – not to crack the wind of the poor phrase,
Running it thus – you'll tender* me a fool.
(*make me look like)

....

Hamlet [about Rosencrantz and Guildenstern]: Then you live
about her waist, or in the middle of her favours?
Guildenstern: Faith, her privates we.

As You Like It

Touchstone: the truest poetry is the most feigning.*
(*feign= pretend, fain= desire; thus questioning the funda-
mental nature of poetry)

The Merchant of Venice

Portia [feigning anger about the missing ring she gave her intended, Bassanio]:
I will ne'er come in your bed
Until I see the ring.*
(*symbol of fidelity, but also sexual organs)

Gratiano: [when the whole story of Portia's and Nerissa's rings has been explained] :
I'll fear no other thing
So sore as keeping safe Nerissa's ring.*
(*the jealousy and anxiety over who has got the ring have the resonance of issues of sexual fidelity and control over spouses)

Romeo and Juliet

Sampson: I will show myself a tyrant. When I have fought with the men, I will be cruel with the maids, and cut off their heads.
Gregory: The heads of the maids?
Sampson: Ay, the heads of the maids, or their maidenheads; take it in what sense thou wilt.

Tis not so deep as a well, nor so wide as a church door, but tis enough, 'twill serve. Ask for me tomorrow and you shall find me a grave man

THOMAS HOOD

1799–1845

However critics may take offence, A double meaning has double sense

Thomas Hood was born in London at a publishing house named Vernor, Hood and Sharp. His father was the Hood of the partnership and his mother was the daughter of another member of the firm. He was a cheerful man, despite constant ill health, and his apparently light verse often had a deeper meaning, conveying his feelings about life for the poor in London at the time. His paternal family were Scottish farmers, but he was proud to be a Londoner, once saying: 'Next to being a citizen of the world, it must be the best thing to be born a citizen of the world's greatest city.' His son, Tom Hood, was also a popular humorist and playwright.

Hood had a private schoolmaster until the age of 14, when he worked briefly in a counting house, but he soon started to study engraving instead. Because of ill health he was sent to relations in Dundee, Scotland, where he made many close friends and led a healthier, outdoor life. It was here that he began to write poetry and had his first writing published.

Practical Joker

An inveterate practical joker, Hood once told his wife to order some plaice from a regular supplier. He warned her to decline any fish that had the 'appearance of red or orange spots, as they are a sure sign of an advanced stage of decomposition'. The unfortunate stooge, Mrs Hood, therefore refused the fish and Hood was greatly amused at his wife's total ignorance at the normal appearance of the fish. Surely, you might think, a woman should know her pla(i)ce?

Hood undertook the publication of the *Comic Annual* from 1830, where he caricatured the leading events and characters of the day, and wrote on contemporary issues, often with an undercurrent of sympathy for the subjects he was meant to lampoon. Readers could, however, be distracted by the incessant use of puns. Hood wrote in vindication:

> *However critics may take offence,*
> *A double meaning has double sense.*

One of the most important issues in his time was grave robbing and the sale of corpses to anatomists. With typical black humour he wrote:

> *Don't go to weep upon my grave,*
> *And think that there I be.*
> *They haven't left an atom there*
> *Of my anatomie.*

Probably the best known of Hood's poems has its title in the last line:

No sun – no moon!
No morn – no noon –
No dawn – no dusk – no proper time of day.
No warmth, no cheerfulness, no healthful ease,
No comfortable feel in any member –
No shade, no shine, no butterflies, no bees,
No fruits, no flowers, no leaves, no birds! –
November!

Some of the poems seem surprisingly modern and his use of puns is always clever, and sometimes mischievous. In his poem *To Henrietta, on her departure for Calais*, the French get some bad press courtesy of Hood. The poem forms a letter to Henrietta, the daughter of his friend, William Harvey, the engraver and artist.

You'll have to learn a chou is quite another sort of thing
To that you put your foot in; that a belle is not to ring;
That a corne is not the knobble that brings trouble to your toes,
Nor peut-être a potato, as some Irish folks suppose.

But pray, at meals, remember this, the French are so polite,
No matter what you eat and drink, 'whatever is, is right'!
So when you're told at dinner time that some delicious stew
Is cat instead of rabbit, you must answer, 'Tant mi-eux'!

Further examples of Hood's humorous wordplay follow:

To Minerva

My temples throb, my pulses boil,
I'm sick of Song and Ode, and Ballad –
So, Thyrsis, take the Midnight Oil
And pour it on a lobster salad.

My brain is dull, my sight is foul,
I cannot write a verse, or read –
Then, Pallas, take away thine Owl,
And let us have a lark instead.

The Bridge of Sighs

One more Unfortunate,
Weary of breath,
Rashly importunate,
Gone to her death!
Take her up tenderly,
Lift her with care;
Fashion'd so slenderly,
Young, and so fair!

Faithless Nelly Grey

Ben Battle was a soldier bold,
And used to war's alarms:
But a cannon-ball took off his legs,
So he laid down his arms!

Faithless Sally Brown

His death, which happen'd in his berth,
At forty-odd befell:
They went and told the sexton, and
The sexton toll'd the bell.

The Irish Schoolmaster

He never spoils the child and spares the rod,
But spoils the rod and never spares the child.

LEWIS CARROLL

1832–1898

Take care of the sense and the sounds will take care of themselves

Lewis Carroll was the pen name of the Reverend Charles Lutwidge Dodgson. He was a mathematics don at Christ Church College, Oxford, who wrote several papers and treatises under his own name. Also a devout Deacon of the Church of England, he coined the pen name Carroll from a Latin form of his first names; Carolus Ludovicus. Among his other interests were inventing, theatre, opera, word and chess puzzles and photography. One of his inventions was a Nyctograph, a device to allow him to make notes in bed at night, without having to get out and find a light. He is credited, however, with making a portable chess set for travellers and a number of word games, including an early form of Scrabble and word ladders, still popular today, where you change one word into another in a number of stages. All in all, you could say he was a bit of a conundrum. He was a little eccentric and once, as a child, gave some worms in the garden weapons to defend themselves with against bird attacks.

He was a shy, stuttering man who found great pleasure in writing nonsense stories, where he applied strict logic to ridiculous situations – probably the reason why his stories and poems have appealed to young and old alike. Today, however, children have the benefit of the modern treatment of his humour in cartoon, drama and simplified versions. He was at his happiest in the company of young girls and we are told that this obsession was entirely innocent. He once wrote: 'I am fond of children (except boys).' This may have been due to him being the oldest of eleven children whose mother died when the youngest was only five. His photographic skills were used to take pictures of children, often naked, in true Victorian style, which would, today, be considered dubious to say the least. He was once described as prim, fastidious and cranky. Perhaps he was just a bachelor, celibate but happy.

Alice's Adventures in Wonderland

Carroll's literary successes came about because of his association with the three daughters of the Dean of Christ Church. His favourite was Alice Pleasance Liddell, the middle sister. On long afternoons spent together, he would tell stories which the three girls asked him to write down. *Alice's Adventures Under Ground* was presented as a Christmas present. This was later expanded and illustrated for publication under the name of *Alice's Adventures in Wonderland* in 1865. *Through the Looking Glass and What Alice Found There* was published in 1872.

Carroll's puns were not usually of the one-line variety, so you need to read them in context for full effect, although lines such as the following from *Alice's Adventures in Wonderland* and based on a proverb stand alone:

Take care of the sense and the sounds will take care of themselves.

He corresponded by letter with children all over the world, sending them poems, puzzles and secret messages. At home he entertained friends with magic shows and paper tricks. Carroll's stories were witty and full of word plays, mathematical twists and political caricatures. They worked on different levels, like all the best children's books do. Adults enjoyed the word play, puns and parody, such as the following verse:

> *Twinkle, twinkle, little bat!*
> *How I wonder what you're at!*
> *Up above the world you fly,*
> *Like a tea tray in the sky.*

This was apparently written about Bartholomew Price, the Professor of Natural Philosophy at Oxford University, called 'Bat' because he was always hurtling from one place to another to attend to one of his many responsibilities. Children were able to understand the logic puzzles with all their twists and turns and enjoy a book which didn't try to improve them or moralize. Jokes were inserted specifically for the sisters for whom they were written, as in the example below about the girls who lived in a well (Lacie is an anagram of Alice). At the chaotic Mad Hatter's tea party in *Alice's Adventures in Wonderland* the Dormouse is cajoled into telling a story.

The Mad Hatter's Tea Party

'Once upon a time there were three little sisters' the Dormouse began in a great hurry; and their names were Elsie, Lacie and Tillie; and they lived at the bottom of a well'.

'What did they live on?' said Alice, who always took a great interest in questions of eating and drinking.

'They lived on treacle' said the Dormouse, after thinking a minute or two.

'They couldn't have done that, you know,' Alice gently re-marked. 'They'd have been ill'

'So they were,' said the Dormouse; 'very ill.'

'But they were in the well,' Alice said to the Dormouse, not choosing to notice this last remark.

'Of course they were,' said the Dormouse: 'well in'.

The Mock Turtle –
from *Though the Looking Glass*

'When we were little,' the Mock Turtle went on at last, more calmly, though still sobbing a little now and then, 'we went to school in the sea. The master was an old Turtle--we used to call him Tortoise--'

'Why did you call him Tortoise, if he wasn't one?' Alice asked.

'We called him Tortoise because he taught us,' said the Mock Turtle angrily: 'really you are very dull!'

Performing Sums – from *Through the Looking Glass*

'And you do Addition?' the White Queen asked. 'What's one and one and one and one and one and one and one and one and one and one?'

'I don't know,' said Alice. 'I lost count.'

'She can't do Addition,' the Red Queen interrupted. 'Can you do Subtraction? Take nine from eight.'

'Nine from eight I can't, you know,' Alice replied very readily: 'but -- '

'She can't do Subtraction,' said the White Queen. 'Can you do Division? Divide a loaf by a knife -- what's the answer to that?'

'I suppose -- ' Alice was beginning, but the Red Queen answered for her. 'Bread-and-butter, of course.

Jabberwocky

For the sheer joy of word play and for firing the imagination of children throughout successive generations, what could be better than *Jabberwocky*, which appeared in *Through the Looking Glass*:

> *Twas brillig, and the slithy toves*
> *Did gyre and gimble in the wabe:*
> *All mimsy were the borogoves,*
> *And the mome raths outgrabe.*

WILLIAM ARCHIBALD SPOONER

1844–1930

You have hissed all of my mystery lectures

A distinguished Anglican warden of New College, Oxford, and, therefore, somewhat cosseted and protected by his comfortable, academic background, the Reverend William Archibald Spooner 'enjoyed' a certain notoriety amongst his students and fellow dons, as a result of his nervous condition which sometimes led him to mix up his words, producing comic or absurd effects, known as 'spoonerisms'. For example, instead of complaining to a lazy student: 'You have missed all of my history lectures', Spooner was alleged to have trilled: 'You have hissed all of my mystery lectures', thus sacrificing any attempt to be stern and put the miscreant in his place, conjuring up instead a silly but definitely amusing image of the wayward student irreverently blowing raspberries at the reverend. The full version of this spoonerism, at the end of the section, shows how Spooner goes on to compound his gaffe still further and raise even more smiles.

Spoonerisms

Unsurprisingly, although there are very few spoonerisms genuinely attributable to the man who mumbled and stumbled across this popular form of word play, there is no shortage of so-called original spoonerisms – doubtless made up by amused students and colleagues, keen to extract the maximum level of humour from seemingly unconscious slips of the tongue. We have all tried our hand – or tongues – at deliberately transposing or reversing letters or syllables of words to produce our own versions.

One of the many unauthenticated spoonerisms of William Spooner: Is the bean dizzy? (dean busy) – found an echo in Oxford in 1968. When student demonstrations had led to many students having to face disciplinary measures; scrawled on the wall of New College, Spooner's old haunt, was the slogan 'Deanz meanz finez', mimicking the then popular TV advertisement for Heinz beans:

A million housewives every day
Pick up a tin of beans and say:
Beanz meanz Heinz.

Authentic spoonerisms, attributed to the Reverend William Archibald Spooner:

- The Kinquering Congs Their Titles Take. ('conquering kings', referring to a hymn)

- The weight of rages will press hard upon the employer. ('rate of wages')

Other spoonerisms attributed but not authenticated:

- A blushing crow.

- A nosey little cook.

- A well-boiled icicle. (well-oiled bicycle)

- I remember your name perfectly, but I just cannot think of your face.

- Is it kisstomary to cuss the bride?

- Someone is occupewing my pie. Please sew me to another sheet. (occupying my pew...show me to another seat)

- The Lord is a shoving leopard.

- Three cheers for our queer old dean! (Queen Victoria)

- You have hissed all my mystery lectures. You have tasted a whole worm. Please leave Oxford on the next town drain. (missed...history, wasted...term, down train)

Other exponents of spoonerisms:

- I'd rather have a bottle in front of me than a frontal lobotomy. (Dorothy Parker)

- I would rather have a free bottle in front of me than a pre-frontal lobotomy. (Dean Martin)

- He's a shining wit. (Barry Cryer, describing a certain media personality)

OSCAR WILDE

1854–1900

Nothing succeeds like excess

Oscar Fingal O'Flahertie Wills Wilde was an Irish writer and prominent aesthete, who became one of the most popular playwrights in London during the early 1890s, as well as one of the most notorious members of Victorian society. He had broad interests, a flamboyant mode of dress and a sharp wit, which many have since tried to emulate. Somewhat ahead of his time, Wilde died prematurely following glittering literary success, imprisonment and financial ruin.

You could hardly say that Wilde came from an ordinary Irish background – extraordinary would be nearer the mark. Born in Dublin, he was the second of three children born to Sir William Wilde and Jane Francesca Wilde. His father, a leading surgeon and a philandering philanthropist, found time for a love of Irish archaeology and peasant folklore, as well as for fathering three other, illegitimate children. His mother was also a writer and a life long Irish nationalist. She had a keen interest in the neo-classical revival and the house was adorned by paintings and busts of ancient Greece and Rome.

Brilliant Student

Until he was nine, Wilde was educated at home, where guests from the medical and cultural scene were frequent. He was introduced to modern languages by a French maid and a German governess. He later won a scholarship to read classics at Trinity College, Dublin, from 1871 to 1874. One of his tutors there, J. P. Mahaffy, inspired his interest in Greek literature. Mahaffy took credit for having created Wilde, but in later life recalled him as 'the only blot on my tutorship'. Wilde was a brilliant student and an active member of The University Philosophical Society. Perhaps this allowed him to pun about the 18th-century philosopher Immanuel Kant: 'Immanuel doesn't pun, he Kant.' On graduating, he went to Magdalen College, Oxford, from 1874 to 1878.

At Oxford, Wilde applied to join the Oxford Union, but failed to be elected. Instead he joined the Apollo Masonic Lodge and was soon raised to the Sublime Degree of Master Mason. Brought up as a protestant, he seriously considered converting to Catholicism, but this only came about on his death bed. At Magdalen, Wilde wore his hair long and decorated his rooms with peacock feathers, flowers, blue china and other objets d'art. One of his mentors at Oxford was Professor Walter Pater, although Wilde's rather flippant devotion to aestheticism was given a purpose through the other great influence at the time, Professor John Ruskin. Ruskin felt that art should link to a better society and to greater moral good. In November 1878, Wilde graduated with a double first in Classical Moderations and Literae Humaniores (Greats).

Rise to Fame

After university Wilde moved into fashionable cultural and social circles in London. At a time when aestheticism was caricatured by Gilbert and Sullivan in *Patience* (1881), Richard D'Oyly Carte invited Wilde on a lecture tour of North America to publicise *Patience* and allow him to sell his image to the American public. A four month tour lecturing on the English Renaissance in Art stretched to a year and on his return to England he began work as a journalist. He married Constance Lloyd in 1884 and the couple had two sons, Cyril (1885) and Vyvyan (1886). Wilde was said to be an adoring father. The opportunity to combine art and social themes drew Wilde into writing drama. In 1891 he wrote *Salome* in French but it didn't make the stage, as it depicted characters from the Bible. Wilde set out to irritate society with his dress and conversation, then to outrage it with the novel, *Dorian Gray*, where vice is hidden beneath art. He finally found his way with *Lady Windermere's Fan*, first performed in 1892. Under the surface of a witty comedy, he hid subtle subversion. In *A Woman of No Importance*, in 1893, he wrote a comedy around illegitimate births and mistaken identities.

The Importance of Being Earnest

Wilde was well-known for his use of puns to soften caustic observations and satire. He described work as the 'curse of the drinking classes.' Extremely popular with society audiences, he found less peace with conservative critics. *The Importance of Being Earnest*, first performed in 1895, is perhaps his most famous play; the title itself is a pun. One of its most famous lines is: 'To lose one parent, Mr Worthing, may be regarded as a misfortune; to lose both looks like carelessness'.

Meanwhile, an intimate friendship had developed between Wilde and Lord Alfred Douglas. Wilde was said to be infatuated and they had a tempestuous affair. Wilde made the mistake of suing Douglas' father, the Marquis of Queensbury, for libel. The outcome was inevitable; Wilde lost the case and was convicted of gross indecency with other men and imprisoned for two years hard labour. On his release he fled to Paris, where he died, destitute at the age of only 46.

On marriage

- Women give to men the very gold of their lives; but they always want it back in small change.

- In married life, three is company, two is none.

- The proper basis for a marriage is mutual misunderstanding.

- A little sincerity is a dangerous thing, and a great deal of it is absolutely fatal.

- The book of life begins with a man and woman in a garden; it ends with revelations.

- Bigamy is having one wife too many, monogamy is the same.

On himself

- The only thing worse in the world than being talked about is not being talked about.

- When I had to fill in the immigration papers, I gave my age as 19, and my profession as genius; I added that I had nothing to declare except my talent.

- I have put my genius into my life, whereas all I have put into my work is my talent.

- I can resist everything except temptation.

- I have very simple tastes, I am always satisfied with the very best.

- Whenever people agree with me, I always feel I must be wrong.

- One half of the world does not believe in God, and the other half does not believe in me.

- Praise makes me humble, but when I am abused I know I have touched the stars.

- I shall have to die, as I have lived, beyond my means.

- To regain my youth I would do anything in the world, except take exercise, get up early, or become respectable.

- This wallpaper will be the death of me; one of us will have to go.

On life

- It is a very sad thing that nowadays there is so little useless information around.

- Ignorance is a rare exotic fruit; touch it, and the bloom, has gone.

- The English country gentleman galloping after a fox – the unspeakable in pursuit of the inedible.

- Democracy is simply the bludgeoning of the people for the people by the people.

- I find that alcohol, taken in sufficient quantities, produces all the effects of intoxication.

- Consistency is the last refuge of the unimaginative.

- A man cannot be too careful in the choice of his enemies.

The proper basis for a marriage is mutual misunderstanding

HECTOR HUGH MUNRO: SAKI

1870–1916

I always say beauty is only sin deep

Hector Hugh Munro is better known by the pen name of Saki. He was one of the earliest writers of the 20th century to break away from sentimental comedy in favour of satire and black humour. He was influenced in his writing by Oscar Wilde, Lewis Carroll, and Rudyard Kipling but is considered the master of the short story. His work has also been compared with the writing of Dorothy Parker. *The Open Window* was famous at the time and nicely summed up the sentiment of the tale in the last line: 'Romance at short notice was her speciality.' This referred to the 15-year-old girl, left to entertain a guest while awaiting the rest of the household's arrival. The poor guest was a nervous wreck to start with, but after listening to her melodramatic stories about why the window was left open, he fled in terror.

Sent to England

Munro was born in Burma, where his father, Charles Augustus Munro, was an inspector-general for the Burmese police. In 1872 his mother, Mary Frances Mercer, died on a visit to England. Charles Munro sent his three children to England, to be brought up by their grandmother and aunts in an overwhelmingly austere household. Happily, this appeared to have little lasting effect on Hector, whose stories seemed elegant enough and somewhat frivolous, but were bitingly satirical and revealed his deep contempt for Edwardian values and society. He later used the characters of the women in the house as the model for many fictional characters in his stories. He went to Pencarwick School in Exmouth and to Bedford Grammar School. When his father returned to England, they travelled a little in Europe. In 1893, he joined the Indian Imperial Police and was posted to Burma but returned two years later because of failing health caused by malaria. He started his career as a journalist, writing for newspapers such as the *Westminster Gazette*, *Daily Express* and *The Morning Post*.

No one is really sure where the name Saki comes from, although it seems likely to have been chosen as a reference to the cupbearer in the poem, the *Rubáiyát of Omar Khayyam*. In his first published collection (1904), *Reginald*, Munro mentioned the character in a piece called 'Reginald on Christmas Presents'. It seems less likely that he chose his nom de plume in honour of the small, long-tailed Amazonian monkey, even though his stories often featured animals. Other works included plays, a study of the Rise of the Russian Empire, published under his own name, and satires such as *The Westminster Alice* (a Parliamentary parody of *Alice's Adventures in Wonderland*).

Death by Sniper

Munro worked as a foreign correspondent for *The Morning Post*, from 1902 to 1908, in the Balkans, Warsaw, Russia and

Paris before settling in London. At the outbreak of World War I, Munro joined up as a soldier in the Royal Fusiliers but refused a commission – he was 43, officially too old and suffering from ill health. He was sheltering in a shell crater on the Western Front in France, in November 1916, when he was killed by a German sniper. Several sources say that his last words were: 'Put that bloody cigarette out!' How ironic that the verbal sharp shooter should be silenced by a sniper.

On gossip

- Hating anything in the way of ill-natured gossip ourselves, we are always grateful to those who do it for us and do it well.

- Scandal is merely the compassionate allowance which the gay make to the humdrum. Think how many blameless lives are brightened by the blazing indiscretions of other people.

- A little inaccuracy sometimes saves tons of explanations.

Wise words

- The people of Crete unfortunately make more history than they can consume locally.

- There may have been disillusionments in the lives of the medieval saints, but they would scarcely have been better pleased if they could have foreseen that their names would be associated nowadays chiefly with racehorses and the cheaper clarets.

- In baiting a mousetrap with cheese, always leave room for the mouse.

- I always say beauty is only sin deep.

- The cook was a good cook, as cooks go; and as good cooks go, she went.

- Poverty keeps together more homes than it breaks up.

- No one has ever said it, but how painfully true it is that the poor have us always with them.

- Addresses are given to us to conceal our whereabouts.

On human nature

- The young man turned to him with a disarming candour, which instantly put him on his guard.

- Children with Hyacinth's temperament don't know better as they grow older; they merely know more.

- Waldo is one of those people who would be enormously improved by death.

- It's no use growing older if you only learn new ways of misbehaving yourself.

- The young have aspirations that never come to pass, the old have reminiscences of what never happened.

- He's simply got the instinct for being unhappy highly developed.
- Children are given to us to discourage our better emotions.

- We all know that Prime Ministers are wedded to the truth, but like other wedded couples they sometimes live apart.

Give a man a
free hand and
he'll run it all
over you

W. C. FIELDS

1880–1946

Now don't say you can't swear off drinking; it's easy. I've done it a thousand times

Despite a distinctly unpromising start in life, including a curtailed education and a particularly troublesome relationship with his father, W. C. Fields showed remarkable resilience and drive throughout his career, persevering until he achieved international recognition as an entertainer, comedian, screenwriter and film star. Born William Claude Dukenfield, on 29 January 1880, in Darby, Pennsylvania, USA, he was the eldest of the five children of British immigrant James Dukenfield and his American wife, Kate Felton, from Philadelphia.

His mere four years of schooling were soon forgotten, as he took up his first paid employment, helping his father sell vegetables from a horse-drawn cart. An alcoholic, James Dukenfield frequently clashed with his strong-willed son, who quickly developed the self-preserving habit of storming out of the house and disappearing to his grandmother's home. Despite the fact that he appeared successfully in musicals later in his career, Fields always blamed his drunken father's caterwauling for his own lack of appreciation of music. Even more damaging, of course, his father's bouts of violence lead-

THE LITTLE BOOK OF PUNS

ing Fields eventually to execute the following, acid comment with apparent levity: 'I am an expert on electricity. My father occupied the chair of applied electricity at the state prison.'

The Distinguished Comedian

By the time he was thirteen, Fields had honed his physical skills and powers of concentration, proving to be an accomplished pool player and juggler. Indeed, his dexterity and personality soon earned him a job as an entertainer at an amusement park in Norristown, Pennsylvania, where his appeal grew, thanks largely to his comic technique of pretending to lose the things he was still juggling. He spent the next 5 or 6 years building his reputation as a comedian and, by the age of nineteen, billed as 'The Distinguished Comedian', he was already commanding impressive fees in halls and theatres across the country. The onset of the new century saw him flourishing as an entertainer and, on 8 August 1900, he married Harriet Hughes. Hattie soon became his partner in his juggling act. Fields could juggle or balance with consummate ease and he delighted in making his mother-in-law, whom he loathed, distinctly uneasy by nonchalantly balancing on his head a lit cigar, a candlestick and candle or a beer bottle, throughout the entire meal. Eventually, he was inducted into the Juggling Hall of Fame.

Although Hattie was already an integral part of the juggling act, Fields insisted she return home to his parents when she fell pregnant in 1903. It proved to be a critical separation, their relationship seemingly failing to survive the remainder of Fields' tour. On his return home, Hattie decided they could no longer succeed as a couple, if he insisted on continuing with his prolonged absences on tour. He rejected the suggestion that he should find himself a day job, for the sake of the family. However, Hattie refused to give him a divorce, and they separated in 1904. In the years that followed she started trying to turn her son against his 'uncaring' father, a ploy which ultimately failed, as predicted by Fields. He refused to speak out against his wife and her unreasonable behaviour, quite possibly prompting his own witticism: 'Never cry over spilt milk, because it may have been poisoned.' Despite his public protestations to the contrary: 'Anyone who hates children and animals can't be all bad' and 'Ah, the patter of little feet around the house. There's nothing like having a midget for a butler'. He always supported his family, irrespective of the size of his earnings, and fellow performers later spoke of his warmth and affection for his children. He also had another son later with girlfriend Bessie Poole – William Rexford Fields Morris was born on 15 August 1917. Although he and his son rarely saw each other over the years, before Fields died in 1946 he was delighted to meet his first grandson, W. C. Fields III.

Developing His Act

In 1903, before the birth of his son, Fields opened at the Palace Theatre in London, and performed alongside Sarah Bernhardt at Buckingham Palace. Then he transferred to Paris, where he took a starring role at the Folies-Bergères, accompanied on the bill by a youthful Charles Chaplin and Maurice Chevalier. But by the time he reached his mid-30s, his career – and his lifestyle – took a dramatic turn. Early on in vaudeville he used to juggle in silence, adding visual comedy to give his act its original stamp. Naturally, he needed total concentration in order to apply his sophisticated skills, but the profession implicitly also demanded, if not abstinence, then at least only moderate consumption of alcohol. Now his addition of verbal humour to his repertoire was, apparently, soon accompanied by frequent references to alcohol, whether or not his actual levels of consumption had increased accordingly. Anecdotal evidence has it that nobody ever saw him drunk and uncontrollable. Significantly, he gave up boozing for more than a year, when he lost a friend in an alcohol-related death, which might well have prompted a relatively rare insight into the evils of drinking to excess: 'Abstaining is favorable both to the head and the pocket.'

More significantly, however, his period of abstinence did come to an end and he resumed his imbibing … and his wisecracks: 'Reminds me of my safari in Africa. Somebody forgot the corkscrew and for several days we had to live on nothing but food and water.' His monologues were liberally doused with references to his appreciation for a tipple or ten, from culinary quotations – 'I cook with wine, sometimes I even add it to the food', to his version of in vino veritas, with his own (in)take on the philosophy of Descartes: 'I drink therefore I am.'

Finally, squeezing the last drops out of this particular bottle, there is a medical condition associated with alcoholism that bears his name, 'W. C. Fields syndrome', revealed by rosacea of the nose and technically termed rhinophyma. Some, however, attributed the famous nose to a family trait.

Film Career

His first feature film, *Pool Sharks*, was released in 1915 and, starting from that same year, he also featured in all of the Ziegfeld Follies until 1921. Two years later he starred in the critically acclaimed musical *Poppy*. Then, in 1925, the film version of the musical, entitled *Sally of the Sawdust*, showcased Fields successfully reprising his starring role. He went on to make a total of 37 feature films. From 1939 his films were self-penned, generally portraying the then familiar, hard bitten, hard drinking, downbeat, pessimistic, almost misogynistic and child-loathing individual he pretended to be throughout his career as an entertainer. When, following several serious illnesses, including bouts of pneumonia, he died of a stomach haemorrhage on Christmas Day, 1946, in Pasadena, California, you could almost hear him incanting (or decanting?): 'Drown in a cold vat of whiskey? Death, where is thy sting?'

On reading the Bible

► Just looking for loopholes.

► I admit I scanned it once, searching for some movie plots . . . but I found only a pack of wild lies.

On women and relationships

- After two days in the hospital, I took a turn for the nurse.

- Ah, yes, Mae West – a plumber's idea of Cleopatra...

- It was a woman who drove me to drink, and I never had the courtesy to thank her for it.

- Some things are better than sex, and some are worse, but there's nothing exactly like it.

- Marry an outdoors woman. Then if you throw her out into the yard on a cold night, she can still survive.

On booze

- Somebody left the cork out of my lunch.

- I never drink water because of the disgusting things that fish do in it.

- I never drink water. I'm afraid it will become habit-forming.

- I gargle with whiskey several times a day, and I haven't had a cold in years.

- Now don't say you can't swear off drinking; it's easy. I've done it a thousand times.

- There are only two real ways to get ahead today – sell liquor or drink it.

- The best thing for a case of nerves is a case of Scotch.

- I never worry about being driven to drink; I just worry about being driven home.

- If I had to live my life over, I'd live over a saloon.

On politics, society and the USA

- The cost of living has gone up another dollar a quart.

- I never vote for anyone. I always vote against.

- Hollywood is the gold cap on a tooth that should have been pulled out years ago.

- A rich man is nothing but a poor man with money.

- I am free of all prejudices. I hate everyone equally.

- The world is getting to be such a dangerous place, a man is lucky to get out of it alive.

- I once spent a year in Philadelphia, I think it was on a Sunday.

Offering advice

- The best cure for insomnia is to get a lot of sleep.

- Don't worry about your heart, it will last you as long as you live.

- The clever cat eats cheese and breathes down rat holes with baited breath.

- The laziest man I ever met put popcorn in his pancakes so they would turn over by themselves.

- Horse sense is the thing a horse has which keeps it from betting on people.

- There comes a time in the affairs of man when he must take the bull by the tail and face the situation.

- If there's a will, prosperity can't be far behind.

ROBERT BENCHLEY

1889–1945

The freelance writer is paid per piece or per word or perhaps

Robert Benchley was a writer, critic and entertainer who wrote about the everyday, idiosyncratic trials of life. He was born in Massachusetts, the son of Charles and Maria Benchley. His older brother Edmund was killed in the Spanish-American War and this had a profound effect on the nine-year-old Robert, influencing his pacifist views. The event was made worse by his mother, who on hearing the news unthinkingly cried out in front of him: 'Why couldn't it have been Robert?'

Robert Benchley married Gertrude Darling, his high school sweetheart in 1914. Nathaniel was born the following year and Robert Jr, in 1919. Nathaniel also had a successful career as a writer and one of his sons, Peter Benchley, wrote the book and screenplay for the film *Jaws*.

Vanity Fair

Benchley graduated from Havard in 1912. During his first term he listed the six things he had learned, the first of which was: 'Charlemagne either died, or was born or did something with the Holy Roman Empire in 800.' At Harvard he gained a reputation as a witty after-dinner speaker. On graduating he moved to New York, landing a job at *Vanity Fair*, where he famously shared an office with Dorothy Parker and became a member of the Algonquin Round Table, along with his friend and fellow Harvard alumnus, Robert E. Sherwood, who was also employed at *Vanity Fair*.

To take Benchley's humour at face value and to chuckle at his one-liners is easy, but there were many facets to his art. He often came across as inept and incapable of functioning in the modern world without support, as if he was struggling to cope with human foibles and felt that inanimate objects often got the better of him. In reality there was an underlying quality to his work which showed his high intellect, biting satire and love of the ridiculous. Like a lot of clever people, he didn't appear to have to work at it. In common with Dorothy Parker, he was self deprecating, although he didn't have the mixed ethnic background of Parker or of many of their contemporaries. He gave the appearance of being surprised by his success: 'It took me fifteen years to discover that I had no talent for writing, but I couldn't give it up because by that time I was too famous.'

Satire and Parody

Sherwood, Parker and Benchley became close friends and conspirators, after many a long lunch at the Algonquin Hotel. When visiting Dorothy Parker in hospital after her attempt to slash her wrists, he quipped: 'Dottie, if you don't stop this sort of thing, you'll make yourself sick'. When the magazine's managers went on a European trip, the three took advantage of the situation by writing satirical articles and parodies on topics such as the effect of Canadian hockey on United States fashion. When the management introduced late slips for staff, Benchley wrote an elaborately crafted excuse which involved a herd of elephants on 44th Street. When Parker was sacked, Benchley resigned. Parker called this 'the greatest act of friendship I'd ever seen'. When the news broke, Alexander Woollcott from *Time* was at a lunch with Benchley, Parker, and others. The three amigos later went to work at *Life* together. Freelance offers understandably began pouring in and he worked hard while claiming to be lazy. He allegedly submitted a magazine piece titled 'I Like to Loaf' two weeks late with an explanatory note: 'I was loafing'. Benchley covered theatre for *Life* and worked for *The New Yorker*, which started in 1925 under the control of Harold Ross, another member of the Round Table. Benchley tackled issues ranging from the problems of careless reporting to European fascism, at the same time showing his versatility by producing regular columns and essays on a range of off-beat subjects. Some of these were later published in collections such as *Pluck and Luck* (1925) and *My Ten Years in a Quandary*, and *How They Grew* (1936). He wrote erudite parodies of the works of Oscar Wilde, Proust and Shakespeare. One example of the latter was a satire on the overly picky academic critic, who deconstructs the text to the point that it falls apart. It was called *Shakespeare Explained: Carrying on the system of footnotes to a silly extreme*. One stage direction and a line of dialogue, where every word was asterisked, included ten footnotes and ran to about four pages. Another of his specialities, which has been much imitated, was his version of programme notes and opera synopses for concert audiences who had no idea what the singers were actually singing about. They would know even less if they took it seriously.

In *Holt! Who goes there?* a piece about the reliance of young mothers on Dr Emmett Holt's *The Care and Feeding of Children*, Benchley showed his fatherly side. This extract on bathing a baby will ring true with any parent or grandparent:

Q: What should the parent wear while bathing the child?
- A rubber loin-cloth will usually be sufficient, with perhaps a pair of elbow-guards and anti-skid gloves. A bath should never be given to a child until at least one hour after eating (that is, after the parent has eaten).

Q: What are the objections to face-cloths as a means of bathing children?
- They are too easily swallowed, and after six or seven wet face-cloths have been swallowed, the child is likely to become heavy and lethargic.

Q: Under what circumstances should the daily tub-bath be omitted?
- Almost any excuse will do. The bathroom may be too cold, or too hot, or the child may be too sleepy or too wide-awake, or the parent may have lame knees or lead poisoning. And anyway, the child had a good bath yesterday.

Benchley's career took a sudden turn in 1922, after he performed an act called 'The Treasurer's Report', which parodied a man bungling his way through a report while standing in for a friend at a social club AGM. Irving Berlin saw it and persuaded him to perform it in the Broadway show *Music Box* – every night for nine months. He later made this into a film, along with another 45 or so short films. One of these, *How to Sleep*, showing Benchley turning restlessly in bed in his pyjamas, earned him an Oscar in 1935. He also appeared in comic roles in a number of feature films, including Alfred Hitchcock's thriller *Foreign Correspondent* (1940), and the 1946 Bing Crosby and Bob Hope comedy, *The Road to Utopia*. After 1943 his film career foundered somewhat, as a result of being too busy, and his alcoholism worsened. As a young man he had been teetotal, but he died in 1945 of cirrhosis of the liver.

On Being a Writer

► The biggest obstacle to professional writing is the necessity for changing a typewriter ribbon.

► The freelance writer is a man who is paid per piece or per word or perhaps.

► After an author has been dead for some time, it becomes increasingly difficult for his publishers to get a new book out of him each year.

- A great many people have come up to me and asked how I manage to get so much work done and still keep looking so dissipated.

- Great literature must spring from an upheaval in the author's soul. If that upheaval is not present then it must come from the works of any other author which happens to be handy and easily adapted.

- I do most of my work sitting down; that's where I shine.

- I have been told by hospital authorities that more copies of my works are left behind by departing patients than those of any other author.

On Drinking

- Why don't you get out of that wet coat and into a dry martini?

- Drinking makes such fools of people, and people are such fools to begin with that it's compounding a felony.

- A real hangover is nothing to try out family remedies on. The only cure for a real hangover is death.

- I know I'm drinking myself to a slow death, but then I'm in no hurry.

On Life

- There seem to be no lengths to which humorless people will not go to analyze humor. It seems to worry them.

- In a house where there are small children the bathroom soon takes on the appearance of the Old Curiosity Shop.

- Tell us your phobias and we will tell you what you are afraid of.

- The surest way to make a monkey of a man is to quote him.

- You might think that after thousands of years of coming up too soon and getting frozen, the crocus family would have had a little sense knocked into it.

- I have tried to know absolutely nothing about a great many things, and I have succeeded fairly well.

- At fifteen one is first beginning to realize that everything isn't money and power in this world, and is casting about for joys that do not turn to dross in one's hands.

- Behind every argument is someone's ignorance.

GROUCHO
MARX

1890–1977

Women should be obscene and not heard

Undisputed master of the quicksilver tongued put-down, 'Groucho' was born Julius Henry Marx, on 2 October 1890 in New York. Despite his desire to continue his education, the bookish 14-year-old Julius, gifted with a fine soprano voice, began his career with a group called the LeRoy Trio. Before long he and his singing brothers became aware of their own comic potential and soon found themselves together in vaudeville. Groucho's trademark loping gait, cigar, glasses, exaggerated greasepaint moustache and eyebrows drew attention immediately to the smart-mouthed insults, observations, sarcastic comments and asides that were the currency of his comedy. Posturing ladies of society were his favourite target, the more so when they objected with horror and disdain at the irrepressible, grinning, eyebrow-twitching little cynic refusing to kowtow to the status the rest of society accorded them.

Shock Tactics

Huge success on Broadway from the mid 1920s – the enormously popular and successful (but relatively silent) juggler and entertainer, W. C. Fields, complained that theirs was the only act he found impossible to follow – soon translated into films, in the vanguard of talking movies. Groucho, the garrulous, innuendo-loving quickwit, was in his element, spreading comic mayhem whenever he could wheedle his way into social circles full of tongue-tied turkeys ready for plucking. Quips such as: 'I've had a perfectly wonderful evening. But this wasn't it', 'Remember you're fighting for this woman's honor – which is probably more than she ever did', and 'She's afraid that if she leaves, she'll become the life of the party', would draw gasps of dismay from fellow players and admiring guffaws from the audience.

Although the flourish of classic films in the early 1930s, including *Monkey Business*, *Horse Feathers* and *Duck Soup*, brought increased fame and wealth, the films grossed successively lower receipts and the Hollywood adventure petered out. However, Groucho had other irons in the fire, working as a radio comedian and show host until well into the 1940s. Having ridden on the crest of the wave of talkies in the 1930s, in the 1950s he was in the right place at the right time again, with the advent of popular television shows. Hosting *You Bet Your Life*, Groucho, while interviewing the quiz contestants, would run amok, ad libbing at the expense of all and sundry within comic range. Later – not quite hoist by his own petard – he would suffer from having been too successful with his comic insults, complaining that when he really did intend his barbs to strike home his intended targets always took it as a joke and laughed it off, much to his annoyance.

Although much of his television and film work from the 1960s onwards proved eminently forgettable, Groucho was able to comfort himself with the knowledge that he and his brothers lived long enough to be rediscovered and reach new, equally admiring audiences. In 1972 his appearance at Carnegie Hall was a sell-out and he accepted on behalf of the Marx Brothers and Margaret Dumont a special Academy Award, in 1974.

Married and divorced three times, between February 1920 and December 1969, Groucho fathered three children – Arthur and Miriam with Ruth Johnson and Melinda with Kay Marvis. He spent his last few years with companion Erin Fleming, finally succumbing to pneumonia, in August 1977. Doubtless fully aware of his inevitable, indelible influence on future generations, he had already prepared his ironic parting shot: 'Why should I care about posterity? What's posterity ever done for me?'

On women, marriage and relationships

- Women should be obscene and not heard.

- Anyone who says he can see through women is missing a lot.

- A man's only as old as the woman he feels.

- Here's to our wives and girlfriends...may they never meet!

- How do I feel about women's rights? I like either side of them.

- I was married by a judge. I should have asked for a jury.

- I wish you'd keep my hands to yourself.

- Madam, before I get through with you, you will have a clear case for divorce and so will my wife.

- Marriage is the chief cause of divorce.

- Marriage is a wonderful institution...but who wants to live in an institution?

- If I hold you any closer, I'll be on the back of you.

Insults, put-downs and telling it straight(ish)

- I didn't like the play, but then I saw it under adverse conditions – the curtain was up.

- I could dance with you till the cows come home. On second thoughts, I'd rather dance with the cows till you came home.

- From the moment I picked your book up until I laid it down I was convulsed with laughter. Someday I intend reading it.

- I never forget a face, but in your case I'll be glad to make an exception.

- She got her good looks from her father. He's a plastic surgeon.

- Now there's a man with an open mind – you can feel the breeze from here!

Self-deprecation ... or naked self-promotion?

- If you want to see a comic strip, you should see me in the shower.

- I've been around so long, I knew Doris Day before she was a virgin.

- I'm 42 around the chest, 52 around the waist, 92 around the golf course and a nuisance around the house.

- Please accept my resignation. I don't want to belong to any club that will accept me as a member.

- Those are my principles. If you don't like them I have others.

Politics, war, business and life

- Military justice is to justice what military music is to music.

- Military intelligence is a contradiction in terms.

- Politics is the art of looking for trouble, finding it, misdiagnosing it and then misapplying the wrong remedies.

- Politics doesn't make strange bedfellows, marriage does.

- I made a killing on Wall Street a few years ago...I shot my broker.

- Blood's not thicker than money.

FRAGILE
4
FRAGILE
4
FRAGILE
KIPPERED
HERRING
KIPPERED
HERRING

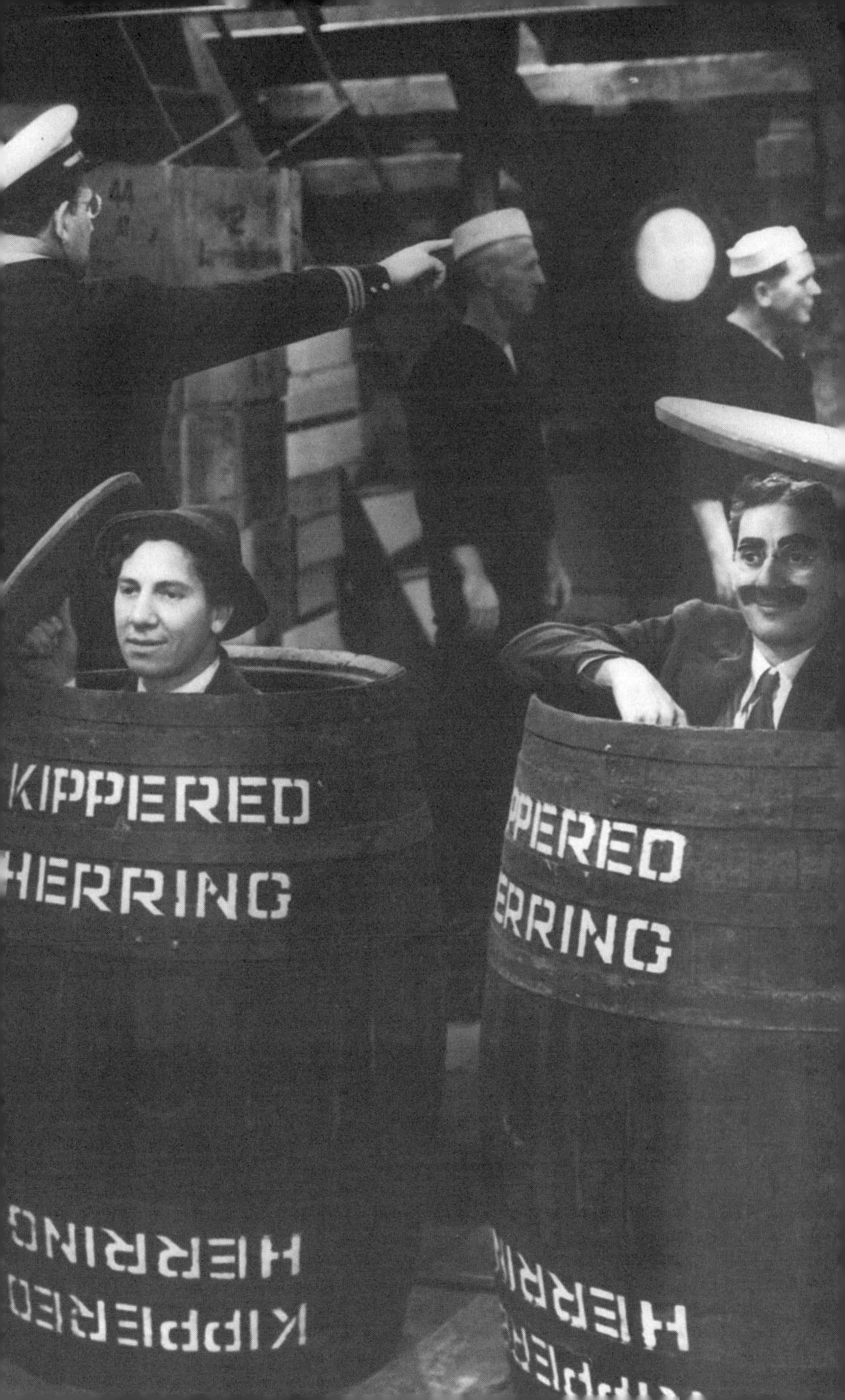
KIPPERED
HERRING
PPERED
ERRING

MAE WEST

1893–1980

I speak two languages, Body and English

If ever anyone's career embodied the maxim that 'there is no such thing as bad publicity', then it must surely have been the life and times of Mae West, American actress, playwright, screenwriter and sex symbol, born Mary Jane West on 17 August 1893, in Brooklyn, New York, USA. Conversely, the gales of protest, the sheer outrage and moral indignation at Mae West's 'obscene' utterances, alongside the ever-growing audiences and popularity ratings, reflected either a deeply divided society or a nation-wide streak of hypocrisy. Worst of all for her, it definitely signalled an official failure to acknowledge fully her abundant talents: the disarming wit, originality and sheer panache of a woman prepared to stand her ground and both defend and promote her controversial views, particularly regarding sex. Accordingly, no-one could ever have the front to label her a shrinking violet: 'I'll try anything once, twice if I like it, three times to make sure.' And what an entertainer and mistress of language!

Whatever the truth of the matter, we can rest assured that from the outset West knew what she was about and understood how to deflect criticism and attempts to undermine her career. As she once stated, in one of her many comments about her favourite subject, men: 'Every man I meet wants to protect me. I can't figure out what from.' Doubtless, the respective qualities of her father, prizefighter 'Battlin' Jack West', turned policeman turned private investigator and her doting mother, Matilda, for whom Mae could never do anything wrong, imbued her with such confidence and presence. The precocious young Mae appeared in amateur shows and often won prizes in talent contests, from the age of seven. Then she launched her professional career in vaudeville, in 1907, at the age of 14.

Issues with Censorship

Following several Broadway shows and revue performances, she decided to strike out on her own, writing plays under the pen name of Jane Mast. *Sex*, the first play she wrote, produced, and directed, also marked her first starring role on Broadway. It went down a storm with the public, but kicked one up with critics and officials, who had the theatre raided and West and the entire cast arrested. It's easy to imagine her pleading: 'It's hard to be funny when you have to be clean', and comparing a court of law with theatre: 'I enjoyed the courtroom as just another stage but not so amusing as Broadway.' Less plausible was her later take on censorship: 'Right now I think censorship is necessary; the things they're doing and saying in films right now just shouldn't be allowed. There's no dignity anymore and I think that's very important.' Irony or a genuine volte-face, when confronted by increasingly explicit material on film and TV? Suffice to say that, in 1927, she was jailed for 10 days for 'corrupting the morals of youth', with two days off for good behaviour – plus untold increase in wealth and fame: 'I believe in censorship. I made a fortune out of it.'

Although her next play, *The Drag*, focusing on homosexuality, was prevented from reaching Broadway, she went on to produce a string of hits, most prominent of which was *Diamond Lil*, in 1928, all still courting controversy for their sexual content and non-conformist attitudes. Some might say she got all she deserved, but many would surely have sympathised when she complained: 'If I asked for a cup of coffee, someone would search for the double meaning.' In fact, she herself offered a telling insight into the real reasons behind moralizing, official bodies' objections to her work, namely, her defiance and insistence upon challenging accepted norms: 'It isn't what I do, but how I do it. It isn't what I say, but how I say it, and how I look when I do it and say it.' Did she ever tire of all this scrutiny and nagging criticism? Apparently not, as long as she continued coming up with wisecracks such as: 'Ten men waiting for me at the door? Send one of them home, I'm tired.' Not exactly the fatigue of a battle-weary campaigner. On the other hand, given her seemingly voracious appetite for men and controversy, wasn't she being a little too clever, denying herself further indulgence, when she defiantly declared: 'A dame that knows the ropes isn't likely to get tied up'?

W. C. Fields

Within three years of signing up with Paramount Pictures, in 1932, Mae West had hit the jackpot, commanding an enormous and ever-increasing income. Her association with

Paramount ended in 1937 but, in 1939, she struck gold again with W. C. Fields in the Universal Pictures film, *My Little Chickadee*, featuring many a memorable line, not least: 'Why doncha come up and see me sometime?' Apart from the box office failure of her next film, *The Heat's On*, in 1943, West abandoned film making until 1970. Meanwhile, her controversial radio show appearances had already assured that she would be banned from the airwaves until 1950 for 'allowing impurity to invade the air'. Good to know she was losing neither her touch nor her propensity to offer sister members of the fairer sex sound advice on how to appeal and win against all the odds: 'Cultivate your curves – they may be dangerous but they won't be avoided.'

1950 also marked the year, as Mae West was nearing 60, that Billy Wilder offered her the role of Norma Desmond, in *Sunset Boulevard*. Only later did he realise the folly of his ways: 'The idea of Mae West was idiotic because we only had to talk to her to find out that she thought she was as great, as desirable, as sexy as she had ever been.' It is undeniable that Mae West herself had clear views on her own worth and on love: 'I never loved another person the way I loved myself.' However, whether conceited, self-deceiving or just utterly self-contained, one attribute she certainly had was sufficient self-knowledge to decline the role. For a woman who was so vociferous about her men and their sexual prowess, West was surprisingly secretive about marriage. At age 17, she married Frank Szatkus (stage name Frank Wallace), in 1911 in Milwaukee, but denied it off and on, eventually revealing that they had only cohabited for a number of weeks, prior to their official divorce decree on 7 May 1943. Confirmation of rumours of another marriage, to Guido Deiro, around 1914, would, of course, have meant that she had committed bigamy. They were certainly lovers, but in her autobiography she simply referred to him as 'D'. Their relationship ended in 1916. Meanwhile, her whole career long was studded, should we say, with men, relationships and controversy.

In 1959, she released her autobiography, entitled *Goodness Had Nothing to Do with It*, which went on to become a best seller. As she had already claimed: 'I always say, keep a diary and someday it'll keep you.' Not that she had ever needed to be a kept woman – in the financial sense, at least. When Mae West's career in cinema reached a natural end, following a few notable failures, she still continued with stage performances at home and abroad. She even released rock and roll albums, promoting them and her usual brand of humour on television and radio. Despite her continued public appearances, West's health began to decline in the 1970s, especially her eyesight. Eventually, she suffered a stroke, then, following the onset of diabetes, a second stroke left her partially paralysed. She died on 22 November 1980, aged 87, at the end of an eventful and richly rewarded career full of challenges, which she not only met defiantly but actually relished, embracing them voluptuously and gracing them – doubtless many years earlier – with her own eloquent, stirring epitaph: 'Too much of a good thing can be wonderful.'

On censorship

- Those who are easily shocked should be shocked more often.

- Virtue has its own reward, but no sale at the box office.

- It ain't no sin if you crack a few laws now and then, just so long as you don't break any.

On virtue, wicked women and sex

- I used to be Snow White, but I drifted.

- I generally avoid temptation unless I can't resist it.

- Sex is emotion in motion.

- She's the kind of girl who climbed the ladder of success wrong by wrong.

- I like restraint, if it doesn't go too far.

- I've been in more laps than a napkin.

- To err is human, but it feels divine.

- It is better to be looked over than overlooked.

- I've been things and seen places.

- When choosing between two evils, I always like to try the one I've never tried before.

- When I'm good I'm very, very good, but when I'm bad, I'm better.

➤ I didn't discover curves, I only uncovered them.

On men

➤ When women go wrong, men go right after them.

➤ It's not the men in my life that count, it's the life in my men.

➤ His mother should have thrown him out and kept the stork.

➤ Save a boyfriend for a rainy day - and another, in case it doesn't rain.

➤ I only have 'yes' men around me. Who needs 'no' men?

➤ I only like two kinds of men, domestic and imported.

➤ A hard man is good to find.

➤ A man in the house is worth two in the street.

On love and relationships

➤ Look your best - who said love is blind?

➤ Love conquers all things except poverty and toothache.

➤ Love isn't an emotion or an instinct - it's an art.

➤ Love thy neighbor - and if he happens to be tall, debonair and devastating, it will be that much easier.

- Marriage is a great institution, but I'm not ready for an institution.

- Opportunity knocks for every man, but you have to give a woman a ring.

- The best way to hold a man is in your arms.

- A woman in love can't be reasonable - or she probably wouldn't be in love.

- All discarded lovers should be given a second chance, but with somebody else.

- Don't keep a man guessing too long - he's sure to find the answer somewhere else.

- Don't marry a man to reform him - that's what reform schools are for.

- Give a man a free hand and he'll run it all over you.

- He's the kind of man a woman would have to marry to get rid of.

mae
WEST
"I'm no Angel"

CARY GRANT
DIRECTED BY WESLEY RUGGLES
A Paramount Picture

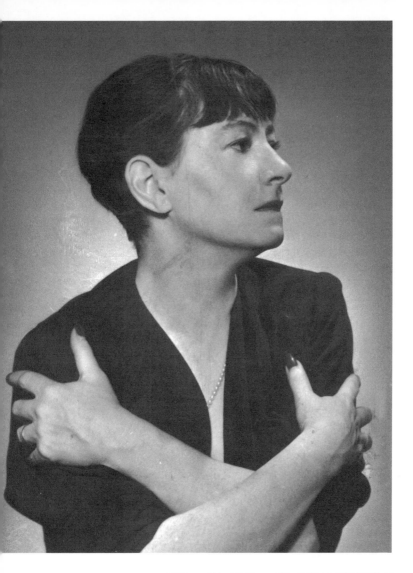

DOROTHY PARKER

1893–1967

I'd rather have a bottle in front of me, than a frontal lobotomy

Dorothy Parker was born Dorothy Rothschild to Jacob Henry and Elizabeth Annie Rothschild in New Jersey on 22 August 1893. This famous American author, poet and satirist had an unhappy childhood, which probably contributed to her sharp wit and scornful view of romantic relationships. She lost her mother at the age of five and detested her father, later accusing him of physical abuse. Her father remarried a strict Catholic named Eleanor Francis Lewis, although Dorothy refused to call her anything other than 'The Housekeeper'.

Despite being of Jewish descent Dorothy was sent to a Catholic Elementary School but her education ended prematurely at the age of 13, when she claimed she was asked to leave after describing the Immaculate Conception as 'spontaneous combustion'. By 1913 both her father and stepmother had died and she earned a living by playing the piano at a dancing school whilst working on poetry in her spare time. She sold her first poem to *Vanity Fair* a year later and eventually began to stand in for P. G. Wodehouse as theatre critic. For someone not particularly keen on theatre, this provided Parker with the perfect opportunity to show off her skills as a master of the carefully crafted put-down.

Fred Crowinshield, the managing editor of *Vanity Fair*, said that Parker had 'the quickest tongue imaginable, and I need not say the keenest sense of mockery'. Writing as 'Constant Reader' in *The New Yorker*, she reviewed A. A. Milne's *The House at Pooh Corner* with the words: 'Tonstant Weader fwowed up', a sarcastic reference to how she perceived Milne to be dumbing down the English language for children.

In 1919 Parker's career really began to take off. She was appointed drama critic at *Vanity Fair* at the same time as Robert Benchley became managing editor and Robert Sherwood was appointed as a writer. Together with other writers and critics, they founded the Algonquin Round Table, a literary clique that helped to cement her place in the annals of history.

The Algonquin Round Table

The Algonquin Hotel was New York's most prestigious literary hotel and the home of a group of young, talented, hard partying writers. Other members included Harold Ross, editor of *The New Yorker*, playwright and director George S. Kaufman and the critic and journalist Alexander Woollcott. Woollcott later described Parker as 'a combination of Little Nell and Lady Macbeth'. Members met almost daily for luncheons at the hotel, where they exchanged banter and played games. At first the group called itself 'The Board' and their lunches were 'Board meetings', until a waiter named Luigi served them, when they became the 'Luigi Board'. Finally they settled on 'The Vicious Circle'. One game was called 'I'll give you a sentence'. A word would be given for the members to incorporate into a humorous sentence. Challenged with the word 'horticulture', Parker came up with the now famous contribution of: 'You can lead a horticulture, but you cannot make her think.'

The Round Table set Parker up with numerous contacts in the literary world and as her star rose higher, so her reputation for witty one-liners grew. Despite this she remained hugely self-deprecating. She once said: 'I'm never going to accomplish anything; that's perfectly clear to me. I'm never going to be famous. My name will never be writ large on the roster of Those Who Do Things. I don't do anything. Not one single thing. I used to bite my nails, but I don't even do that any more.' Behind closed doors she struggled with alcoholism, depression and three marriages. After separating from her first husband, Edwin Parker, whom she had married in 1917, she had some affairs, notably one with playwright Charles MacArthur. An aborted pregnancy led to depression and her first attempt at suicide. She apparently remarked 'How like me, to put all my eggs into one bastard'. She divorced Edwin in 1928. She made two more attempts at suicide and reflected on them in a poem, *Resumé* which was published in a collection entitled *Enough Rope*:

> *Razors pain you,*
> *Rivers are damp,*
> *Acids stain you,*
> *And drugs cause cramp,*
> *Guns aren't lawful,*
> *Nooses give,*
> *Gas smells awful,*
> *You might as well live.*

A Star is Born

The book became a bestseller and was followed with *Sunset Gun* (1928), *Death and Taxes* (1931), and *Not So Deep as a Well* (1931). Her poems were dry, sardonic and elegant takes on love, relationships and the shallowness of modern life. In the 1930s she moved with her second husband, Alan Campbell, to Hollywood and found that it epitomized everything she disliked about the world. Over the next years she and Campbell worked on 15 film scripts together and she contributed to the screenwriting of *A Star is Born* (1937), which won an Oscar for Best Original Story. Despite this success, she was disdainful about work which kept her from more serious literary engagements and a growing awareness of politics. Marriage with Campbell was tempestuous and they divorced in 1947, only to remarry in 1950. They lived apart for much of the rest of Campbell's life and he died of a drugs overdose in 1963. Over the next decades Parker became more vocal on civil liberties and civil rights. She helped found the Hollywood Anti-Nazi League in 1936 and chaired the Joint Anti-Fascist Rescue Committee. She saw less and less of the Round Table friends and her friendship with Robert Benchley was strained. Parker met S. J. Perelman at a party in 1932, and after a rocky start they remained friends for over 30 years.

In 1944 Parker worked with Woollcott to produce an anthology of her short stories and poems entitled *The Portable Dorothy Parker*. Parker's book has the distinction of being the only 'Portable' other than the works of William Shakespeare and The Bible to remain continuously in print. Parker was blacklisted as a Communist in 1950 during the McCarthy era and died alone in a hotel in 1967. She left her entire estate to Martin Luther King Jr. She dismissed much of her work as 'just a little Jewish girl trying to be cute', but decades after her death, many still regard her as one of the most shrewdly funny satirists of the 20th century. Her most enduring love, her love of language, stayed with her until the end. When asked to suggest an epitaph for herself she suggested: 'This one's on me'.

On Booze

- I'd rather have a bottle in front of me, than a frontal lobotomy.

- One more drink and I'd have been under the host.

On Literature

- This is not a novel to be tossed aside lightly; it should be thrown with great force.

- The only 'ism' Hollywood believes in is plagiarism.

- (On the office she shared with Robert Benchley): One cubic foot less would have constituted adultery. (They called it the Parkbench)

- A little bad taste is like a nice dash of paprika.

- (On the death of Calvin Coolidge, a man of few words): How do they know?

- (On Katharine Hepburn's performance in The Lake): Miss Hepburn, it seems, had run the whole gamut of emotions from A to B.

- And I'll stay away from Verlaine too; he was always chasing Rimbauds.*
(*This is a play on the title of the popular song 'I'm Always Chasing Rainbows'; Paul Verlaine was the lover of Arthur Rimbaud.)

On Sex and Relationships

- Brevity is the soul of lingerie.

- The transatlantic crossing was so rough, that the only thing I could keep on my stomach was the first mate.

- All I need is room to lay a hat and a few friends.

- If all the girls who attended Yale prom were laid end to end, I wouldn't be a bit surprised.

- Take me or leave me, or, as is the usual order of things, both.

- She was pleased to have him come and never sorry to see him go.

- (Telegram to a friend who had given birth) Dear Mary: We all knew you had it in you.

On Life

- You can't teach an old dogma new tricks.

- A girl's best friend is her mutter.

- Men seldom make passes at girls who wear glasses.

- Salary is no object: I want only enough to keep body and soul apart.

- Money cannot buy health, but I'd settle for a diamond-studded wheelchair.

- Ducking for apples – change one letter and it's the story of my life.

A hole has been found in the nudist camp wall.

The police are looking into it.

TOMMY COOPER

1921 – 1984

Slept like a log last night Woke up in the fireplace

Tommy Cooper was a British comedian and magician. He was a member of The Magic Circle and was famous for his tricks going badly wrong during his act to comic effect. He was a droll comedian and caused immediate amusement with his bulky 6ft 4in (1.93m) frame, topped off with his long straight face, wild hair and trade mark red fez. His bizarre appearance made his audience laugh before he even spoke. Typically Cooper's first line would be a perfectly timed, 'I haven't said anything yet!' causing further paroxysms.

While his on-stage character made his act go wrong for comic purposes, on 15 April 1984, Cooper famously died on television, midway through his live performance. Believing that it was a joke, the audience laughed as he fell, until it became apparent he was seriously ill and had suffered a heart attack.

In a 2005 poll *The Comedians' Comedian*, Cooper was voted the sixth greatest comedy act ever by fellow comedians and comedy insiders. He is commonly cited as one of the best comedians of all time, with several polls placing him at number one.

Early Life

Born in Wales, Cooper grew up in Exeter where at the age of eight an aunt bought him a magic set and he spent hours perfecting the tricks.

Magic ran in his family – his brother opened a magic shop in the 1960s called D. & Z. Cooper's Magic Shop. And in Eastbourne even today, the town to which Tommy Cooper retired, Cooper's Magic Shop in the town centre is run by Tommy's niece Sabrina.

After school, Cooper became a shipwright and in 1940 was called up to serve in World War II. He served initially in the Desert Rats of the British 8th Army in Egypt. Cooper became part of the entertainment party and developed an act around his magic tricks but a lot would go wrong and Tommy made jokes out of his bungling. One evening, during a sketch in which he was supposed to be in a costume having forgotten his hat, Cooper reached out and borrowed a fez from a waiter which got a huge laugh. It was from this incident that two of the trademarks of his later theatre act developed: the ever-present fez and his slapstick comedic failed magic tricks

Act development

When he was demobbed, Cooper took up show business in 1947 and worked variety theatres around the country. Cooper rapidly became a top-liner in variety with his turn as the conjurer whose tricks never succeeded, but it was his TV work which raised him to national prominence. He was popular with audiences for four decades. His many television shows during the mid 1970s made him one of the biggest and most easily recognizable comedians in the world.

Cooper was a heavy drinker and smoker, and experienced a decline in health during the late 1970s, suffering his first heart attack in 1977 while in Rome, where he was performing a show. Three months later he was back on television. By 1980, though, his drinking problem meant that British TV companies would not give him another series.

Cooper's drinking increased and had a devastating effect on his family and nearly ruined his career. Initially he drank to ease the anxiety of going on stage. He said, 'People say I've only got to walk out on stage and they laugh. If only they knew what it takes to walk out on stage in the first place.' But what began as a shot of liquid courage eventually became a psychological crutch and heavy addiction.

Death on a live television show

In 1984, Cooper collapsed from a heart attack in front of millions of television viewers, midway through a live transmission of his act from Her Majesty's Theatre in London. An assistant had helped him put on a cloak for his sketch, while Jimmy Tarbuck, the host, was hiding behind the curtain waiting to pass him different props which he would then appear to pull from inside his gown. Suddenly Cooper's legs gave way and helping hands tried to pull him back through the curtains, but for a long time his size 13 feet protruded poignantly from beneath the closed curtains. This was indeed the final curtain falling on the great man. Meanwhile, frantic efforts were being made backstage to revive Cooper. Paramedics eventually arrived and moved his body to Westminster Hospital where he was pronounced dead on arrival.

While no one can do justice to his unique 'failed' magic tricks, Tommy Cooper's legacy lives on in his famous jokes, puns and one liners. An industry of Cooperisms and punchlines has grown up around this legendary funny man. No one knows for sure if he ever actually said half of them!

Cooperisms

- Police arrested two kids yesterday, one was drinking battery acid, the other was eating fireworks. They charged one - and let the other one off.

- Two aerials meet on a roof - fall in love - get married. The ceremony was average - but the reception was brilliant.

- Doctor doctor, I can't stop singing the 'Green Green Grass of Home'. He said: 'That sounds like Tom Jones syndrome'. 'Is it common?' I asked. 'It's not unusual', he replied.

- I backed a horse last week at ten to one. It came in at quarter past four.

- I'm on a whiskey diet. I've lost three days already.

- A man walks into a bar with a roll of tarmac under his arm and says: 'Pint please, and one for the road.'

- I went to the doctors the other day and I said, 'Have you got anything for wind?' So he gave me a kite.

- My mother-in-law fell down a wishing well, I was amazed, I never knew those things worked.

- A woman has twins, and gives them up for adoption. One of them goes to a family in Egypt and is named 'Amal.' The other goes to a family in Spain, they name him Juan'. Years later; Juan sends a picture of himself to his mum. Upon receiving the picture, she tells her husband that she wished she also had a picture of Amal. Her husband responds, 'But they are twins. If you've seen Juan, you've seen Amal.'

- There's two fish in a tank, and one says 'How do you drive this thing?'

- I went to buy some camouflage trousers the other day but I couldn't find any.

- A jump-lead walks into a bar. The barman says, 'I'll serve you, but don't start anything'

- Slept like a log last night....Woke up in the fireplace.

- A Scotsman, an Englishman and an Irishman walk into a bar. The barman says, 'Is this some kind of joke?'

- A sandwich walks into a bar. The barman says, 'Sorry we don't serve food in here.'

- I cleaned the attic with the wife the other day. Now I can't get the cobwebs out of her hair.

Two TV aerials met on a roof - fell in love - got married. The church ceremony was average but the reception was brilliant.

GEORGE CARLIN

1937–2008

When you step on the brakes your life is in your foot's hands

Both officially, by public acclaim and accolades, and unofficially, by popular demand, George Carlin ranked amongst the greatest of stand-up comedians of all time. He was born 12 May 1937, in New York City, USA, to mother Mary (definitely a Catholic) and father Patrick (more alcoholic than catholic, according to George, who claimed to be an atheist by the time he was 2 and a half years old – an early onset of the age of reason). Despite having to work long hours as a secretary, Mary brought up the two boys, elder brother Patrick and George, on her own, moving from town to town to stay ahead of her estranged but persistent husband.

When he was 17, Carlin decided to drop out of high school and join the US Air Force, training to be a radar technician, in Shreveport, Louisiana. There he also tried his hand at disc jockeying on a local radio station, a move that ultimately signalled his departure from the Air Force before he had completed his training. He also met newsman Jack Burns at the radio station and they went on to work together in nightclubs as a comedy duo from 1960 to 1962. When they went their separate ways, Carlin launched his solo stand-up comedy career and started appearing on television variety shows, most notably *Rowan and Martin's Laugh In*.

Saturday Night Live

George Carlin's popularity grew throughout the 1960s and 1970s. Even the notorious 'Seven Dirty Words' – a comedy routine that became a radio censorship case eventually heard in the US Supreme Court in 1978 – served to raise his profile and status as a stand-up with emphatically expressed views on language, society and customs. In short, it found an echo in his laconic take on political correctness, profanity and censorship: 'The status quo sucks.' He was the first-ever host of NBC's *Saturday Night Live*, on 11 October 1975, as well as the first-ever host of *Fridays* (1980), an ABC programme in the same mould as 'SNL'. The 1980s and 1990s saw him flourishing in stand-up performance, TV sitcoms and appearances and films, and in November 1994 he was inducted into the Comedy Hall of Fame. The new millennium brought more film roles: following his appearance in Kevin Smith's 1999 film *Dogma*, he worked with Smith again, with a cameo appearance in *Jay and Silent Bob Strike Back* (2001) and a bigger role in *Jersey Girl* (2004).

Having previously suffered a heart attack – disappearing from the scene for five years in the mid-seventies – Carlin fell ill again and died of heart failure on 22 June 2008, in Santa Monica, California. Perhaps a fitting epitaph for Carlin, who always retained a highly ironic outlook on life, might spring from one anecdote about his close friendship with Joe Pesci. Unable to resist lampooning religion whilst complimenting his friend, Carlin claimed he prayed to him instead of God 'because he looks like he can get things done' – the kind of irreverence that also prompted him to invent a bogus religion for a newspaper competition: 'Frisbeetarianism is the belief that when you die, your soul goes up on the roof and gets stuck.'

On religion and beliefs

➤ Atheism is a non-prophet organization.

➤ I have as much authority as the Pope, I just don't have as many people who believe it.

➤ The main reason Santa is so jolly is because he knows where all the bad girls live.

➤ I'm not concerned about all hell breaking loose, but that a PART of hell will break loose... it'll be much harder to detect.

➤ By and large, language is a tool for concealing the truth.

➤ When evolution is outlawed, only outlaws will evolve.

On food, drink and relationships

- To be intoxicated is to feel sophisticated, but not be able to say it.

- Give a man a fish and he will eat for a day. Teach him how to fish, and he will sit in a boat and drink beer all day.

- One tequila, two tequila, three tequila, floor.

- The other night I ate at a real nice family restaurant. Every table had an argument going.

- Do infants enjoy infancy as much as adults enjoy adultery?

- Don't sweat the petty things and don't pet the sweaty things.

On phobias, futility and absurdity

- I'm not afraid of heights, I'm just afraid of falling from them.

- Dusting is a good example of the futility of trying to put things right. As soon as you dust, the fact of your next dusting has already been established.

- (On being fired from his Las Vegas lounge act in the early 60s): I was fired for saying 'shit' in a town where the most popular game is called 'craps'.

- There are nights when the wolves are silent and only the moon howls.

- I went to a bookstore and asked the saleswoman, 'Where's the self-help section?' She said if she told me, it would defeat the purpose.

- Well, if crime fighters fight crime and fire fighters fight fire, what do freedom fighters fight?

- What does it mean to pre-board? Do you get on before you get on?

- When you step on the brakes your life is in your foot's hands.

- When you're born you get a ticket to the freak show. When you're born in America, you get a front row seat.

- Fighting for peace is like screwing for virginity.

- Just cause you got the monkey off your back doesn't mean the circus has left town.

- Most people work just hard enough not to get fired and get paid just enough money not to quit.

- Have you ever noticed that anybody driving slower than you is an idiot, and anyone going faster than you is a maniac?

TIM VINE

1967–

Black beauty, now there's a dark horse

Born in London, Tim Vine is a stand-up comedian who uses humorous puns throughout his act. He fires jokes at the audience at such a rate that on 7 October 2004, Vine broke the world record when he told 499 jokes in an hour. He has been nicknamed the Joke Machine Gun as his quick-fire, one-liner wordplay act leaves the crowd aching and groaning more in pain than enjoyment from the extended bout of laughter. He has appeared regularly at Edinburgh Festival Fringe with his shows Punslinger and The Joke-amotive.

Tim Vine has written a great deal of material which is often confused with Tommy Cooper jokes. Unfortunately Vine's jokebook gained notoriety when it was stolen and many of his jokes were then circulated around the world in an email claiming to be Tommy Cooper jokes. Even the London West End show about Tommy Cooper ended up featuring Vine's jokes. Irritated at the time, Vine is now a little bit flattered by the comparison to the great comic magician, although Cooper does not feature as one of Vine's favourites. Instead he cites old-school comics such as Jackie Mason and Frankie Howerd as influences. Phil Silvers also features as one of Vine's fond childhood memories in the *Sgt Bilko* TV show.

Jeremy Vine the journalist and news broadcaster is Tim's older brother. Although the age difference is less than two years, the comedian concedes, 'Jeremy is much more grown up than me.'

In August 2010, Vine won the prize for the funniest joke of that year's Edinburgh Festival Fringe, following a public vote from a judged shortlist. His winning joke was

> *'I've just been on a once-in-a-lifetime holiday.*
> *I'll tell you what, never again.'*

Some well known Tim Vine puns
(you may think that Tommy Cooper wrote them!)

- I went to buy an ice cream. The guy said Hundreds and thousands? I said, Let's start with just one. He said Knickerbocker glory? I said, Yes, I do get a certain amount of freedom in these trousers.

- I wanted to be a milkman, right – but I didn't have the bottle!

- Black beauty, now there's a dark horse.

- One in five people in the world is Chinese. And there are five people in my family. So it must be one of them. It's either mum or dad. Or my older bother Colin. Or my younger brother Ho Chan Chu. But I think it is Colin!

- So I took my dog for a walk and it was really angry – well it's a cross breed!

- I went to the butchers the other day and the butcher said, 'I bet you £5 you can't guess the weight of that meat on the top shelf'. 'I'm not gambling!' I said, 'The steaks are too high!'

- He said, 'I'm going to chop off the bottom of one of your trouser legs and put it in a library'. I thought, 'That's a turn-up for the books.'

- I saw a bargain the other day, a TV set for £1. Only problem was the volume control was stuck on full. Come on, how can you turn that down?

- A guy walks into the psychiatrist wearing only cling-film for shorts. The shrink says, Well, I can clearly see you're nuts.

- The other day someone left a piece of plasticine in my dressing room. I didn't know what to make of it.

- A man came round in hospital after a serious accident. He shouted, Doctor, doctor, I can't feel my legs! The doctor replied, I know you can't, I've cut your arms off.

- So I went to the doctor and he said, 'You've got hypochondria.' I said, 'Not that as well!'

- Advent Calenders. Their days are numbered.

- I met this bloke with a didgeridoo and he was playing Dancing Queen on it. I thought, 'That's abba-riginal.'

- I told my girlfriend I had a job in a bowling alley. She said 'Tenpin?' I said, 'No, permanent.'

So I said to the Gym instructor

"Can you teach me to do the splits?"

He said
"How flexible
are you?"

I said
"I can't make
Tuesdays"

KNOCK KNOCK...

There doesn't seem to be a definitive answer as to where the humble Knock Knock joke began, but many attribute it to Shakespeare's famous tragedy, *Macbeth*. The Bard often provided his audience with some much-needed comic relief after scenes of doom and gloom – the purveyors of these include the Grave Digger in *Hamlet*, the Fool in *King Lear* and the Porter in *Macbeth*.

After the drama of Macbeth's dagger soliloquy, the drunken Porter hears knocking at the gate and imagines the situation were he meets the keeper of the gates of hell; 'Knock knock! Who's there i'the name of Beelzebub? Here's a farmer that hanged himself on the expectation of plenty...' He then goes on to list some of the people he thinks might make it into hell, including an equivocator (conman) who committed treason and a light-fingered tailor.

The Knock Knock joke didn't seem to take off in the form we know today until the 20th century. It was reported in an edition of the *Pittsburgh Post Gazette* from 1936 that a new form of summer parlour game was doing the rounds, but that it was probably just a passing fad that would be gone by autumn! The jokes of this inter-war period took on a political leaning; the following example is a little dig at unsuccessful presidential candidate Alfred Landon who disappeared into obscurity after losing the election.

Knock Knock
Who's there?
Landon!
Landon who?

Knock Knock jokes seem to be most prevalent in English-speaking countries but cross demographic lines into parts of western Europe and beyond. There are cultural variations but most seem to follow the same basic pattern. An example from France goes:

Toc Toc
(knock knock)
Qui est là?
(who's there?)
Sheila
Sheila qui?
(Sheila who?)
Sheila lutte finale!
(It's the final struggle – a pun on *c'est la lutte finale*; the opening line of The Internationale.)

Knock Knock jokes are among the first attempts that children make at humour. In 1950s South Africa, this type of gag was very popular in playgrounds, a favourite being:

Knock Knock
Who's there?
Delores
Delores who?
Delores my shepherd!

There is little doubt that the Knock Knock joke as we know it today isn't particularly sophisticated, but ask the immortal question of most adults and you'll find that most can't resist finding out the name of who's supposedly there.

Knock Knock
Who's there?
Tom Sawyer
Tom Sawyer who?
Tom Sawyer underwear!

· ·

Knock Knock
Who's there?
Amos
Amos who?
Amos-quito!

· ·

Knock Knock
Who's there?
Boo
Boo who?
Don't cry; it's only a joke!

Knock Knock
Who's there?
Aardvark
Aardvark who?
Aardvark a million miles to see
one of your smiles!

. . . .

Knock Knock!
Who's there?
Madame
Madame who?
Madame foot's caught in the
door!

. . . .

Will you remember me
in an hour?
Yes
Will you remember me
in a day?
Yes
Will you remember me
in a week?
Yes

Will you remember me
in a month?
Yes
Will you remember me
in a year?
Yes
Knock Knock!
Who's there?
See? You've forgotten me
already!

. . . .

Knock Knock!
Who's there?
Lettuce
Lettuce who?
Lettuce in and you will find out!

. . . .

Knock Knock.
Who's there?
Hannah
Hannah who?
Hannah partridge
in a pear tree!

Knock Knock
Who's there?
Odysseus
Odysseus who?
Odysseus the last straw!

. . . .

Knock Knock
Who's there?
Tennis
Tennis who?
Tennis five plus five!

. . . .

Knock Knock
Who's there?
Zeke
Zeke who?
Zeke and yee shall find!

Knock Knock
Who's there?
Zombies
Zombies who?
Zombies makes honey, others
are queens!

. . . .

Knock Knock
Who's there?
Abyssinia
Abyssinia who?
Abyssinia when you get back!

DOCTOR,
DOCTOR

According to some accounts, Doctor, Doctor jokes have their origin in the Roman joke book mentioned in the introduction. One of the 260 or so jokes included in it goes as follows:

A doctor was talking to a patient. 'Doctor,' the patient says, 'Whenever I get up after a sleep, I feel dizzy for half an hour, then I'm all right.' 'Then wait for half an hour before getting up', said the doctor.

Inevitably the format of these jokes has evolved a little since then and, like the Knock Knock gag that we all know and love today, the Doctor, Doctor joke relies on a simple exchange between the tried-and-trusted comic convention of the 'silly man' bouncing off the 'straight man'. Why said silly man is the trusted medical professional is open to debate, but there is some method in his madness as this kind of joke has stood the test of time.

The legendary Tommy Cooper was a keen user of the Doctor, Doctor joke and a number of his favourite gags drew on the humour generated by the often awkward exchanges between the physician and his patient; the first couple of jokes here have been attributed to the famous fez wearer.

A woman told her doctor, 'I've got a bad back.' 'The doctor said, 'It's old age.' The woman said, 'I want a second opinion.' The doctor says, 'OK, you're ugly as well.'

Doctor, Doctor, I keep thinking I'm a kleptomaniac.
Hmm, you should take something for that!

**Doctor, Doctor
I can't get to sleep.**

**Sit on the edge of the bed
and you'll soon drop off.**

. . . .

**Doctor, Doctor
I think I'm a bridge.**

What's come over you?

**Several cars, a large
truck and a coach.**

. . . .

**Doctor, Doctor,
I feel like a pack of cards.**

I'll deal with you later.

. . . .

**Doctor, Doctor will this
ointment clear up my spots?**

I never make rash promises!

Doctor, Doctor
When I press with my finger here... it hurts, and here... it hurts, and here... What do you think is wrong with me?

You have a broken finger!

. . . .

Doctor, Doctor
My son has just swallowed a roll of film!

Hmmmm. Let's hope nothing develops.

. . . .

Doctor, Doctor
I feel like a pair of curtains!

Pull yourself together, man!

. . . .

Doctor, Doctor
everyone keeps ignoring me.

Next please!

EDINBURGH FESTIVAL FRINGE
FUNNIEST JOKE AWARD

The 2010 award was judged by eight comedy critics, whose shortlist of 24 jokes went forward to a public vote. Competition organisers said each judge sat through an average of 60 performances, totalling 3,600 minutes of comedy material. They may only have skimmed the surface, however. The Fringe website lists 883 comedy shows taking place during the festival's month-long run.

THE FUNNIEST JOKES AT THE FRINGE

I've just been on a once-in-a-lifetime holiday. I'll tell you what, never again.
Tim Vine

....

I'm currently dating a couple of anorexics. Two birds, one stone.
David Gibson

....

I bought one of those anti-bullying wristbands when they first came out. I say 'bought', I actually stole it off a short, fat ginger kid.
Jack Whitehall

....

As a kid I was made to walk the plank. We couldn't afford a dog.
Gary Delaney

Dave drowned. So at the funeral we got him a wreath in the shape of a lifebelt. Well, it's what he would have wanted.

Gary Delaney

Wooden spoons are great. You can either use them to prepare food. Or, if you can't be bothered with that, just write a number on one and walk into a pub...

Gareth Richards

THE WORST JOKES AT THE FRINGE

Why did the chicken commit suicide? To get to the other side.

Sara Pascoe

You know citycentre beat officers... Well are they police who rap?

Sean Hughes

I made a Battenberg cake where the two colours ran alongside each other. I called it apartheid sponge.

John Luke Roberts

I like to play chess with bald men in the park, although it's hard to find 32 of them.

Emo Phillips

How many Spaniards does it take to change a lightbulb? Just Juan.

Dan Antopolski

Hedgehogs – why can't they just share the hedge?

Antopolski's inclusion in the 'worst joke' list comes just a year after he won the trophy for best joke.

I wondered why the baseball was getting bigger. Then it hit me.

LOADSA PUN –
BEST TABLOID HEADLINES

Crises, whether political, scandalous or sporting, tend to inspire tabloid headline writers to great heights. They do, of course, have a limited time and space to attract attention, so over the years the use of large bold type coupled with half a dozen carefully chosen words has become a finely honed weapon in the constant battle for readership.

The ammunition is the pun. Many headlines are corny, some are crude but most hit the spot and raise a smile as we hand over the money to buy the newspaper.

CLASSIC HEADLINES

Super Caley Go Ballistic, Celtic are Atrocious

Referring of course to the famous Scottish Cup defeat of Glasgow Celtic by First Division Inverness Caledonian Thistle by 3-1 in 2000. It's not exactly a quick fire punch line, but it follows the classic formula: take a song lyric everyone knows, change a few words around and set it in big bold type.

I've been backed

When Arnold Schwarzenegger won the Californian elections.

Headless Body In Topless Bar

The *New York Post's* headline is one of the most famous.

Eighth Army Push Bottles Up Germans

And legend has it that during WWII, after the British cut off a German retreat in Africa, this was the headline back home.

Hawk Kestrel manouevres in the park

The headline accompanying a picture of a Kestrel and a Barn Owl fighting over food.

Shoots you Sir

When Gianni Versace was assassinated in 1997, the *Daily Sport* less than tactfully punned.

Diniz in the Oven

In 1997 Grand Prix driver Pedro Diniz's car caught fire during a race.

Sting's massage in a brothel

Sting got paparazzi'd coming out of a red light district establishment whilst on tour with the Police in Germany.

Sarky gets narky at Carla malarky

Recently, the French leader Nicholas Sarkozy's anger at wife Carla Bruni's affairs.

I want nookie with hookie

A woman wrote into *The Sun* about how she wanted to sleep with the one-eyed, hook-handed convicted terrorist Abu Hamza. *The Sun* gave her headline treatment.

George Michael Shunts Trucker In Rear

After George Michael had a car crash.

For fox sake

When demonstrators protested outside the House of Commons against fox hunting.

And finally ... *The Sun's* headline about French farmers hijacking a lorry of UK lamb:

L'ambush!

APPENDIX

Infamy Infamy! They've all got it in for me!

The pun creates a joke from similar sounding words. It is different to a malapropism or a double entendre, although they can be equally funny.

A malapropism mixes up two expressions, resulting in nonsense.

A double entendre has a hidden rude joke as an intentional second meaning.

Puns, malapropisms and double entendres have long been used for comic effect through the ages by classic writers such as Shakespeare, Sheridan and Oscar Wilde, and more recently have been a standard tool for comedy writers in film and television

Malapropism

The term malapropism was first coined following a 1775 play *The Rivals*, written by Sheridan in which a humorous character, Mrs Malaprop, frequently mixed up her words. She said:

► *Illiterate* this fellow from your memory. (obliterate)

► An *allegory* on the banks of Nile. (alligator)

Shakespeare used mixed up phrases for fun long before Sheridan, but they were named Dogberries after one of his characters in *Much Ado about Nothing*.

Constable Dogberry:

- Comparisons are *odorous*. (odious)

- Sir, we have *comprehended* two *auspicious* persons. (apprehended, suspicious)

Benvolio in *Romeo and Juliet*:

- She will *indite* him to some supper. (invite)

Nick Bottom in *A Midsummer Night's Dream*:

- Lion vile hath here *deflower'd* my dear. (devoured)

Clown in *The Winter's Tale:*

- Hard luck, being in so *preposterous* estate. (prosperous)

Malapropisms often form the basis of cartoons

- 'I'm going to get *tutored*!" (neutered) – One dog bragging to another in a Gary Larson *Far Side* cartoon.

The writers of many well known TV and movie comedies also use malapropisms to raise a laugh.

Some of Archie Bunker's best lines from the US sitcom *All in the Family* were malapropisms :

- Buy one of them battery-operated *transvestite* radios. (transistor)

- Patience is a *virgin*. (virtue)

Stan Laurel in the Laurel and Hardy films malapropped constantly, usually accompanied by a scratch of the head and an emphatic nod:

- We heard the ocean is *infatuated* with sharks. (infested)

- We'd like a room with a southern *explosion*. (exposure)

- The doctor said I might get *hydrophosphates*. (hydrophobia)

- We floundered in a *typhoid*. (typhoon)

- We're just like two peas in a *pot*. (pod)

Here are some other renowned malapproppers:

- He could technically not have penisary contact with her *Volvo*. (vulva) – Tony Soprano, *The Sopranos*

- I know all about reverse *biology*, buddy. I'm not an idiot. (psychology) – Earl Hickey, *My Name Is Earl*

- What are you *incinerating*? (insinuating) – *Steptoe & Son* written by Galton and Simpson

- No, a *moo* point. Yeah, it's like a cow's opinion. It just doesn't matter. It's *moo*. (moot) – Joey Tribbiani, *Friends*

- Good to be back on the old *terra cotta* (terra firma) – Del Boy in *Only Fools and Horses*

We never had no education. You see, we're not illiterate enough

In *Allo 'Allo,* a British World War II comedy set in France, the cast are supposed to be speaking French, but the script is in English with heavy French Clouseau type accents. Officer Crabtree, who is an English undercover agent speaks atrocious French, which is rendered in the series as broken English filled with malapropisms. He recalls a '*nit* on the *bonk* of the Thames' (night, bank) with a female 'secret *urgent*' (agent). Another regular is his greeting when he enters René's Café: 'Good *moaning*' (Good morning)

Double entendre

A double entendre is a phrase devised to be understood two ways. The more obvious meaning is straightforward and harmless, while the second meaning is less so often with a sexual innuendo. A person who is not familiar with the hidden meaning may not get it, apart from seeing that others around them find it funny.

Often, older words or phrases can cause a problem. They may have been innocuous at the time, but today have a more obscene or sexual meaning; such as 'have a gay old time' from *The Flintstones* theme tune song. One possibly intentional example is the character Charley Bates from Charles Dickens' *Oliver Twist*, frequently referred to as Master Bates. The word masturbate had become common at that time and it was seen as an in-joke.

There is a persistent urban legend which created sexually suggestive names for the characters in the children's TV cartoon

Captain Pugwash. Master Bates, Seaman Stains and Roger the Cabin Boy never did appear in the cartoon and the implication that the captain's name was a slang Australian term for oral sex was also false. John Ryan, the creator of *Captain Pugwash*, successfully sued *The Guardian* newspaper in 1991 for printing the story.

Bawdy double entendres, such as: 'I'm the kinda girl who works for Paramount by day, and Fox all night' were the trademark of Mae West, in her early-career vaudeville performances as well as in her later plays and movies.

After World War II in Britain, innuendo humour and double entendres progressively began to filter through during the 1950s and 1960s. Particularly significant in this respect were the *Carry On* series of films.

The *Carry On* films were full of double entendres, slapstick and outrageous acting. However they captured a moment in time in post-war Britain which was distinctly more innocent. That *Carry On* moment may have gone, but the films will always exist. With character names such as Miss Allcock, Dr Carver, Dr Killmore, a gynaecologist named Dr Prodd, the Khazi of Kalibar, Sidney Ruff-Diamond, and Mr Boggs the toilet maker with his assistant Sid Plummer, the *Carry On* films took double entendres to new heights of sauciness. Kenneth Williams' pun: 'Infamy! Infamy! They've all got it in for me!' as Julius Caesar in *Carry On Cleo (1964)* was voted the funniest film one-liner ever.

My God, what's Bond doing?

I think he's
attempting
re-entry, sir

Moonraker (1979)

In the 1970s BBC TV series *Are You Being Served?*, Mrs Slocombe frequently referred to her pet cat as her 'pussy', apparently unaware of how easily her statement could be misinterpreted, such as: 'My pussy got soakin' wet last night. I had to dry it out in front of the fire.' Generally a viewer would be expected to detect the sexual innuendo.

Double entendres are popular in modern movies, as a way to conceal adult humour. The James Bond films are notorious for such 'laddish' humour. In *Tomorrow Never Dies* (1997), Bond says he is busy brushing up on a little Danish when he is secretly in bed with a Danish girl. He is well known as 'a cunning linguist', says Moneypenny. This was taken a stage further by Mike Myers in Austin Powers: 'You may be a cunning linguist, but I'm a master debater!' he said in *Goldmember*. Bond character names come from the the *Carry On* school of casting. Pussy Galore and Holly Goodhead were parodied in Austin Powers as Alotta Fagina and Felicity Shagwell.

In *Pulp Fiction*, Uma Thurman, playing the character Mia Wallace, excuses herself in Jack Rabbit Slim's restaurant from John Travolta (Vincent Vega) to go powder her nose, and subsequently snorts cocaine off the bathroom sink.

Double entendres are also very common in the titles and lyrics of pop songs.

Bob Dylan, in the song *Rainy Day Women* from the *Blonde on Blonde* album, repeats the chorus: 'Everybody must get stoned.' In context, the phrase refers to the biblical punishment of stoning to death, but it also means to get stoned on drugs.

The Rolling Stones had to incorporate many multiple-layered meanings into the song *Brown Sugar* camouflaging its latent sexual sadomasochistic content to avoid a radio and TV ban in 1971. Written by Mick Jagger with his secret black girlfriend Marsha Hunt in mind, the song is a classic Stones dual combination of drugs and girls. These days when the Rolling Stones perform *Brown Sugar* live, Jagger often changes the line, 'Hear him whip the women just around midnight,' to the less offensive, 'You shoulda heard him just around midnight'. Legend has it that the original song title was to be Black Pussy rather than Brown Sugar.

The Tom Petty and the Heartbreakers song *Don't Do Me Like That* is another example of hidden references to sexual intercourse.

An album entitled *Cunning Stunts* was one of the British rock band Caravan's bestsellers in 1975 and includes the track *The Dabsong Conshirtoe*.

The Arctic Monkeys sing, 'the weekend rockstars are in the toilets, practising their lines', in *Fake Tales of San Francisco*. Referring to lines of cocaine.

The Rush album *Moving Pictures* is a well known visual *triple* entendre. The front cover shows furniture removal men who are physically moving pictures alongside people who are crying because the pictures are emotionally 'moving'. The back cover features a film crew making a 'moving picture' of the whole scene.

No reports exist of any quadruple entendres.

I backed a
horse today
at ten to one

It came in at quarter past four